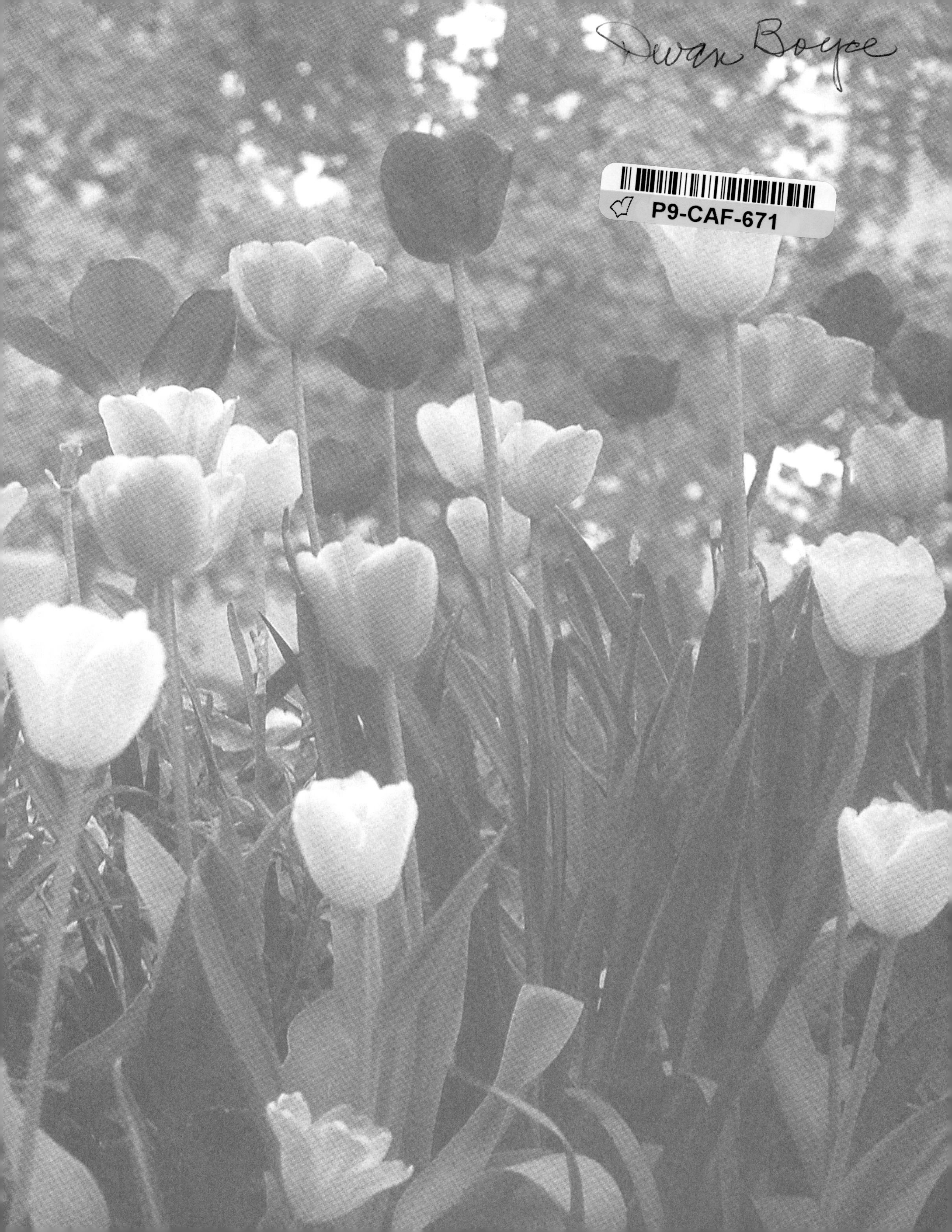

Temple Square
Gardening

Christena Gates, Diane Erickson,
Shelly Zollinger, Larry Sagers

**EAGLE
GATE**

Salt Lake City, Utah

Dedicated to Peter Lassig
and all who make the gardens beautiful

All photographs are copyrighted. For information on specific photographs and their credits and copyright, contact the publisher. We acknowledge Esther T. Henrichsen for her contributions to the history chapter and Peter Lassig for his contributions to the design chapter. We also acknowledge Diane Sagers, garden writer, *Horticulture Plus,* for her review and contributions to the rose chapter and for her rose photographs. Many of the photographs in the Favorite lists and other photographs throughout the book by Larry Sagers. Color wheel diagram by Geoffrey Sagers, Sagers Web Design. Other photographs by Craig Dimond © by Intellectual Reserve, Inc., Richard Erickson, Esther T. Henrichsen, John Luke, and Larry Tavenner. Special thanks to Sheri Dew, Jana Erickson, Michael Morris, and all those who contributed to *Temple Square Gardening.* Front and back cover photographs by Craig Dimond © by Intellectual Reserve, Inc., back cover photographs of grasses and rose, Larry Sagers and Diane Sagers. Design by Richard Erickson. For more photo credits, refer to page 182.

Library of Congress Cataloging-in-Publication Data

Gates, Christena.
   Temple Square gardening / Christena Gates, Diane Erickson, Shelly Zollinger, Larry Sagers
      p.   cm.
   ISBN 1-57008-801-2 (Hardbound : alk. paper)
      1. Gardening—Utah—Salt Lake City.   2. Temple Square (Salt Lake City, Utah)   I. Erickson, Diane.   II. Zollinger, Shelly.
III. Larry Sagers.   IV. Title.

SB453.2.U8 G38 2002
635.9—dc21   2002013911

Printed in the United States of America   42316-6936
Inland Press, Menomonee Falls, WI

10   9   8   7   6   5   4   3   2   1

Contents

Foreword

Anyone who has labored to design or plant a garden at Temple Square can't help but think, "When we build, let us think that we build for ever. Let it not be for present delight, nor for present use alone; let it be such work as our descendants will thank us for, and let us think, as we lay stone on stone [or plant beside plant], that a time is to come when those stones [and plants] will be held sacred because our hands have touched them" (John Ruskin, *The Seven Lamps of Architecture,* New York City: Dover Publications, 1989, 186).

This book is about the standards and processes (some call them secrets) used by the gardeners at Temple Square to achieve, with a variety of plants, gardens of enduring beauty and low maintenance. Our vision has always been to create loveliness that calls attention to the Creator, not the designer, and to produce a sequence of garden scenes that seem right and inevitable and that serve as a tribute to Heavenly Father and his inspired plans to bless mankind.

We learned early as we worked together on the gardens that for gardeners, the year at Temple Square is more than just four seasons; rather, it's closer to fourteen seasons. We learned that we had a fiduciary obligation to our visitors to keep the gardens lovely year-round.

We also learned that conventional gardening plans don't work well because they are two dimensional. They can only be conveniently read right side up, but the gardens they represent are like walk-through sculptures that can be created, experienced, and critiqued from any angle and in any sequence in space and time. Conventional plans also fail to show at a glance how their design fits into a garden's blooming sequence.

We needed a new way of planning that allowed us to create and view a garden from any angle without having to orient the plan to true north. We needed a way of planning that allowed us to create and critique with surgical insights the strengths or failings of any plan. And we needed a planning format that allowed the simplest mind to comprehend a garden's basic organization.

For a new standard of planning, we took our cue from scoring. Music is scored. Dance is choreographed with a score. We decided to do the same in producing our gardens—a process that we share in this book.

Temple Square gardens have always been a joyful collaboration among equals. We have basked in each other's light. The success of the gardens has been a shared process, setting the pattern for the shared authorship of this book. May the wisdom and experience of its authors help you to produce your own garden, with "such work as [your] descendants will thank [you] for."

PETER LASSIG

TEMPLE SQUARE LANDSCAPE DESIGNER

Publisher's Preface

Every year more than a million visitors admire the world-famous gardens that weave through the thirty-five-acre complex known as Temple Square. Among the largest formal gardens in the world, the gardens at Temple Square have received numerous awards for their internationally renowned landscaping and design. From the luminous pastels of spring to the contrasting brilliant tones of late summer and early fall to the grandeur and allure of Christmas, the gardens are beautiful in any season.

Now, for the first time, three talented gardeners at Temple Square, joined by well-known gardener Larry Sagers, share the history of the gardens and give expert gardening advice based on more than fifty years of cumulative experience.

Christena Gates served nine years as director of Garden Tours, a program that provides free tours of the gardens at the Church Office Building plaza and on the Conference Center roof. She is a graduate of the University of Utah, a master gardener, a garden designer on Temple Square, and a lecturer for the Speeches in the Community program, which provides outreach to organizations along the Wasatch Front.

Diane Erickson is director of the Garden Talks in the Park program, a community program sponsored by The Church of Jesus Christ of Latter-day Saints. A garden designer on Temple Square, and lecturer, she is an advanced master gardener and a member of the board of directors for the Davis County Master Gardeners.

Shelly Zollinger, who holds a degree in horticulture, is the owner and operator of Country Garden Design, a landscape design and consulting firm. A full-time employee on the grounds at Temple Square, she is a garden designer, lecturer, and advanced master gardener.

Larry Sagers is well known to Utah residents as the long-time cohost of the *KSL Greenhouse Show,* a weekly radio program for which he has won numerous broadcasting awards. His gardening column has been featured in the *Deseret News* every Sunday for more than a decade. He is a Utah State University Extension horticulturist with an undergraduate degree from Brigham Young University and a master's degree from Utah State University. Larry has served for many years as a consultant to the gardeners at Temple Square.

These four master gardeners have distilled their wide range of knowledge and experience into this useful book, which will appeal to beginner and experienced gardeners alike.

The first few chapters of *Temple Square Gardening* focus on the basics. A gardening primer provides important information on testing and preparing soil, watering, fertilizing, and controlling weeds. This part of the book also explains the factors to be considered in planning a garden, offers instructions for selecting the right varieties of plants, and discusses various garden styles that create a specific mood or feeling.

In subsequent chapters, the authors share unique design methods and color schemes that will help gardeners determine the numbers and types of plants they will need to fill their gardens. And a valuable chapter on spring-flowering plants gives essential tips and suggestions for duplicating the look of Temple Square's famous gardens in a home setting. Chapters on roses, tricks of the trade, and pest and disease management follow.

Temple Square Gardening also features a full-color photographic encyclopedia of nearly four hundred species of plants used on Temple Square. This section contains detailed information on USDA hardiness zone specifications, light requirements, size of plants, and bloom season. Valuable information on the performance of each kind of plant in the Temple Square gardens is included,

along with lists of drought-tolerant plants, low-maintenance plants, plants for shade gardens, and much more.

The last chapter provides helpful listings of some favorite books, magazines, and catalogs used by Temple Square gardeners. It also provides a list of helpful websites that gardeners can use to research additional information, and it offers several educational suggestions.

Full of practical advice to simplify gardening, beautiful photographs to provide inspiration, instructive drawings to help re-create the perfect look, and simple instructions to emulate the pros, this gorgeous book will teach you all you need to know about caring for a beautiful garden in each season of the year. With a wealth of information, ideas, and advice, *Temple Square Gardening* is the perfect sourcebook for turning your home garden into a work of art.

Chapter 1

History of Gardening on Temple Square

When members of The Church of Jesus Christ of Latter-day Saints fled the eastern United States, they brought with them a pragmatic city plan designed by their martyred prophet, Joseph Smith. This "Plat of the City of Zion" drew a distinction between "lots" within the city and "fields" outside of it. The city lots were to be true gardens—enclosed pieces of ground devoted to the cultivation of flowers, fruits, and vegetables. The fields were designated for general farming.

The earliest city ordinance dictated that home lots be enclosed by a fence or wall. City lots included trees such as Lombardy poplars, black locusts, and trees of heaven; lawns of clover that could be scythed (the lawn mower didn't come to Utah until the 1870s); row (furrow) irrigation; undefined edges in the gardens; and swept earth paths.

The city plan called for broad sidewalks and exceptionally wide streets to allow wagons to turn around. No lot was to have more than one house, and the front of the lot was to be planted in a grove, with the remaining property for orchards and gardens. Because of this, Salt Lake City became a garden-plot city in the tradition of medieval Europe, having a commercial character but growing much food within its limits.

With an unusual combination of extensive missionary travel, massive inpouring of immigrants, and strong theocratic encouragement, horticulture grew faster in the Salt Lake Valley than in any other place in America. Missionaries and immigrants brought seeds and plants directly to the valley, skipping the usual route of seed houses and arboreta of the eastern United States.

In *A History of Horticulture in America,* U. P. Hedrick says, "Gardening in Utah progressed by leaps and bounds. . . . It is doubtful that in any other state in the Union the growing of fruits, vegetables, and flowers made such a rapid progress in so short a time."

The Latter-day Saints became plantsmen, and their gardens became noteworthy for their botanical

Temple Square is unique—a large city block with high walls surrounding public gardens. The walls, bordered by rows of trees planted in the 1890s, muffle traffic noises, creating a place of quiet and serenity.

displays. Although the gardens lacked visual design, the juxtaposition of their intense green against barren, severe mountains gave the city an Oriental appearance that many found beautiful and inviting.

Gardening was a religious act in that it contributed to the building up of Zion and evidenced a commitment to the common good. It is particularly unusual, then, that contemporary LDS society, so rich in cultural folklore, lacks any garden lore from this era. No known cultivation superstitions survive from this time, which is known for its

The earliest city ordinance dictated that home lots be enclosed by a fence or wall. This view of South Temple Street shows Brigham Young's residences—the Lion House and the Beehive House.

The pioneers took the semiarid landscape and built a city from scratch. The completed Tabernacle and partially constructed temple can be seen in this 1883 photograph.

legacy of hard work encouraged by Edenic rhetoric and expectations of divine assistance.

Utah was far removed from manufacturing centers, and merchandise was extremely costly. That suited Brigham Young, who wanted a self-sufficient society independent of any reliance on goods from the United States. The boycotting of foreign goods was avidly advocated by Church leaders and was a major factor in the development of a unique style of gardening.

"Some argue that it is too expensive to fence and raise fruit, but it is my business to decorate and beautify Zion, it is part of my religion as much as going to meeting, praying or singing," said Brigham Young (*Deseret News,* 21 August 1855).

The pioneers took the semiarid landscape and built a city from scratch. They did not attempt to imitate nature but rather to make their civilized imprint on it. They had grand ambitions in humble surroundings and were sensitive to their dependence upon the environment. During those times it was rare in America to hear gardening preached from the pulpit, but the Saints were counseled that if they cultivated, "the desert shall . . . blossom as the rose" (Isaiah 35:1).

William C. Staines was among many pioneer gardeners considered "renaissance men" who approached gardening in the valley from a background of horticulture and experience. He joined the Church around 1841 and arrived in the Salt Lake Valley from Nauvoo in September 1847. He imported seeds, executed sophisticated experiments, corresponded with the great plantsmen of Britain and the United States, and managed the horticultural and agricultural societies of the Utah Territory. He was also the caretaker of the gardens and orchards belonging to Brigham Young.

Staines became a partner with his friend, Mr. Letson, in the Pioneer Nursery. They sold gardening tools and pottery and became major suppliers of seeds and plants. One of Staines's last acts was

Long hidden beneath the streets of downtown Salt Lake City, City Creek once again flows above ground, in front of the Conference Center. The creek is edged by a variety of grasses and daylilies. The granite rocks skirting the creek were taken from the original quarry used to supply granite blocks for the Salt Lake Temple and the Conference Center.

Temple Square in the early 1950s reflected the labors of the previous century. Meandering clipped lawns and chinoiserie sidewalks were popular in the Victorian Age. Rows of trees were planted during the City Beautiful Movement of the 1890s, and monuments and fountains date back to the Pioneer Revival Era of the late 1940s.

1. Temple
2. Temple Annex
3. William Staines Conservatory (greenhouse)
4. North gate
5. Center mall
6. Tabernacle
7. Greenhouse
8. West gate
9. Assembly Hall
10. Seagull Monument
11. South gate
12. Bureau of Information
13. Monument
14. Pioneer log cabin
15. East gate
16. Hotel Utah
17. Church Administration Building

Temple Square in the Early 1950s

to deed funds to the Church for the building of a conservatory on Temple Square. The conservatory grew flowers for the Church gardens until it was torn down in 1961.

The gardens of Temple Square became more structured when a master plan was developed after World War II, during the presidency of Heber J. Grant. The Church was growing rapidly and needed more offices and larger buildings.

The block east of Temple Square was home to small offices for the leaders of various Church organizations, the Hotel Utah (now the Joseph Smith Memorial Building), and the Lion and Beehive Houses, both built as private residences. Brigham Young used the building connecting the Beehive and Lion Houses to conduct the early affairs of the Church as well as of the Utah Territory.

In 1971, ground was broken for the Church Office Building, designed by Church architect George Cannon Young to accommodate the offices of the various Church organizations. Young also created a master plan for the block and persuaded Church leaders to include an area that could support gardens of world-class standards.

Young developed the basic garden concept and master plan for the gardens around the buildings to enhance their design. He guided the architectural layout of patios and walkways to designate spaces for gardens. Also involved in the design of the Church Office Building Plaza was Salt Lake landscape architect Karsten Hansen and Hare and Hare, a landscape architect firm in Kansas City. They designed the gardens between the Joseph Smith Memorial Building and the Church Administration Building.

Head gardener Irvin T. Nelson shared in the planning of the gardens and shepherded their development and planting styles. His design ideas were less structured than Young's, and together the two forged a pattern of spaces and concepts

that laid the foundation of the gardens as we know them today.

The early gardens were characterized as Victorian in style but would not have been considered significant in today's gardening world. Individual garden designs were unrelated to each other but reflected the fashions of the day.

Peter Lassig, current landscape designer—or "gardener," as he prefers to be called—began

Zipper borders and floating flower gardens are legacies from the Victorian Age.

The Assembly Hall boasts a summer display of petunias, geraniums, and sweet alyssum.

More than a million people visit Temple Square annually.

Four acres of gardens, with full irrigation, adorn the roof of the Conference Center.

The arrangements within the individual beds at Temple Square are informal and naturalistic.

working on the gardens in 1953 as a teenage assistant under Irvin T. Nelson. When Nelson retired in 1975, Peter took over. He now leads a staff of six head gardeners and various designers who design flower beds in harmony with his philosophy "that the gardens are to be produced within formalized borders that reflect the genius of the Creator, not the designer."

Today the gardens can be found on three blocks located in downtown Salt Lake City—Temple Square, the Church Office Building block, and the Conference Center block. In addition to tending these three blocks, Church gardeners also take care of the Brigham Young Historic Park, the Heber C. Kimball and Brigham Young Cemeteries,

and the areas around the Museum of Church History and Art and the Family History Library. The architectural layout and planting areas of the gardens are structured and formal, but the arrangements within the individual beds look informal and naturalistic.

"The intent is to give a clear sense of purpose to the gardens, which is to lead men to God," Lassig said. "The flowerbeds themselves are spontaneous and include a plethora of flowers to help people appreciate God and to create a setting for man's contemplation of the infinite."

In accordance with this philosophy, the gardens contain informal arrangements within layouts defined by rows of trees, hedges, walkways, patios,

The cedar of Lebanon tree by the east gate of Temple Square was brought from Israel in 1949 as a small seedling.

Columnar English oak trees line the parterre garden between the Joseph Smith Memorial Building and the Church Administration Building. The Church Office Building can be seen in the background.

The Brigham Young Historic Park, east of the Church Office Building, features a display of plants native to Utah as well as an example of row irrigation used by the pioneers.

The Lion House and the Beehive House are surrounded by cottage-style gardens.

and other features. This design creates a sense of order but evokes peaceful relaxation.

The gardens have many significant features. Of particular note is the row of English and American elms planted in the 1890s on each side of the long mall between the north and south gates of Temple Square. The cedar of Lebanon tree by the east gate of Temple Square was brought from Israel in 1949 as a small seedling. The one-foot plant was presented to the Church by Maggie Cottam Petty, who carried it on her lap during a long flight from Israel to Salt Lake City.

In 1987, the columnar English oak trees in the parterre garden between the Church Administration Building and the Joseph Smith Memorial

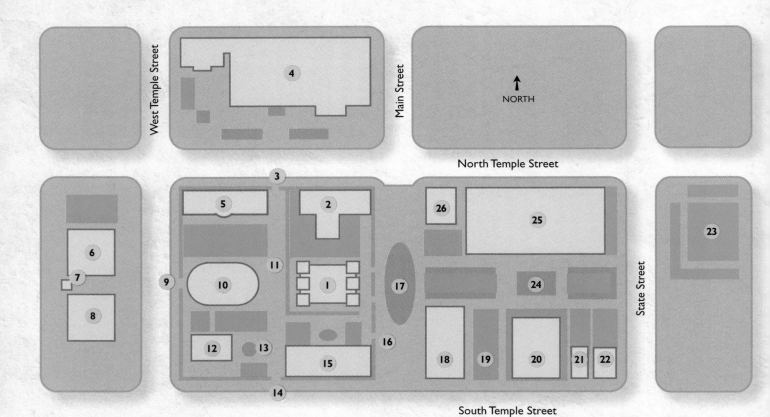

1. Temple
2. Temple Annex
3. North gate
4. Conference Center
5. North Visitors Center
6. Museum of Church History and Art
7. Pioneer cabin
8. Family History Library
9. West gate

10. Tabernacle
11. Center mall
12. Assembly Hall
13. Seagull Monument
14. South gate
15. South Visitors Center
16. East gate
17. Reflection pool
18. Joseph Smith Memorial Building

19. President's Parterre Garden
20. Church Administration Building
21. Lion House
22. Beehive House
23. Brigham Young Historic Park
24. Plaza fountain
25. Church Office Building
26. Relief Society Building

Present-day Temple Square

Building were uprooted, balled, wrapped in burlap, and moved to the Church's greenhouse, where they remained for three years while the Hotel Utah was remodeled into the Joseph Smith Memorial Building. The oaks were then returned and transplanted into shallow soil in the rooftop gardens of the Church Office Building and the Joseph Smith Memorial Building. To aid with the transplanting of such large trees, drip tubing with a fogger was attached to the top of each tree trunk. The drip tubing and fogger were activated intermittently throughout the day to keep the trees cool and help them withstand the transplanting process. Remarkably, no trees were lost.

Other rooftop gardens are located atop the massive Conference Center, which seats 22,000 people. The soil depth in these gardens and in the rooftop gardens of the Church Office Building and the Joseph Smith Memorial Building ranges in most areas between four inches and three feet. The growing medium consists of a sterile product called Utelite, which is produced in Utah. It is used in roof gardens worldwide because it weighs less than average soil and does not compact. It consists of expanded shale cooked at 2,000 degrees Fahrenheit. Peat moss and fertilizer are added to the Utelite, along with a top dressing of mulch after plants have been put in the ground.

Most perennials and annuals used in the gardens are grown at the Church's greenhouse, a relatively small operation that provides about 500,000 plants per year. Most of the pansies planted with bulbs in the fall are grown from seed so designers can use specific color combinations and varieties.

Thirty-four full-time gardeners maintain the current gardens, with assistance from twenty to thirty seasonal gardeners. In addition, about eighty Church service missionaries, called as Garden Guides, serve a minimum of four hours per week working in the gardens and giving garden tours on the Church Office Building block and on the roof

Garden Guides are Church service missionaries who work in the gardens, give garden tours, and serve the community.

More than one thousand volunteers help in the Temple Square gardens each year.

at the Conference Center. Their other duties include giving speeches in the community as well as hosting a gardening program each Wednesday evening in the Brigham Young Memorial Park, located east of the Church Office Building.

Each year the Garden Guides conduct about three thousand visitors on formal tours of the gardens and reach an additional two thousand people through the Speeches in the Community program. About five hundred people annually attend the Speeches in the Park, which run from June through August in the Brigham Young Memorial Park. Various gardening experts are invited to teach about their particular subject.

About fifteen additional Church service

missionaries also help twice a week for four hours each day. They are unique individuals who have physical or mental challenges but who are able to serve in the gardens. Twice a year, in the spring and the fall, more than a thousand volunteers pull out plants and replant the gardens for the next season.

The gardens undergo a complete change every six months, a process that takes about three weeks. They are famous for their spring bulb displays, which are best viewed during April and May. The summer gardens start looking good in June. September and early October are the best months to view the fall gardens. The world-renowned Christmas lights and decorations that cover the three blocks during the Christmas season can be seen from Thanksgiving through the first week of January. More than one million visitors view the lights and decorations each Christmas season.

Over the years, the Temple Square gardens

Temple Square gardens are famous for incredible displays of spring flowers that are best viewed during April and May.

have received numerous awards and citations of merit. Awards of particular significance include the prestigious Award of Excellence from The American Society of Landscape Architects, Utah Chapter, for the Brigham Young Park in 2000; the Civic Beautification Award from the *Salt Lake Tribune* in 1994; and the Downtown Award for Individual Achievement in 1993. In addition, many articles highlighting various aspects of the Temple Square gardens have appeared in national magazines. ❧

In August, workers begin to set up a spectacular array of Christmas lights. The annual display can be observed from Thanksgiving to the first week in January.

Chapter 2

Gardening Basics

SOIL

The "dirt" on gardening is in the soil. Good soil is essential to the success of flower beds. Temple Square gardeners live by the motto, "Poor soil equals poor flowers." The first thing you need to do as you plan your garden is to get to know your soil. You may be lucky and have great soil with good texture, plenty of nutrients, and a pH that will accommodate your plants. But if you're among the many who aren't so lucky, you need to prepare your soil so it can be a great garden host.

Soil is more than dirt. It is a complex mixture of minerals, organic matter (plant and animal residues), air, and water, which combine to serve as a reservoir of oxygen and nutrients. In soil, physical, chemical, and biological reactions constantly take place. This process releases some plant nutrients while making other nutrients less available. Good soil is alive and active as it promotes good plant growth.

'Orange Star' zinnias complement colorful impatiens.

Four Principal Components of soil

Air

Minerals

Water

Organic Matter

An average soil is 5 percent organic matter, 25 percent air, 25 percent water, and 45 percent mineral matter. When Brigham Young said, "This is the right place," he wasn't talking about Utah soil. The pioneers left behind far better soils when they came west.

Other than in streambeds and along some foothills, Utah soils are not rich and fertile. Like the pioneers who settled this area and like the gardeners at Temple Square, you must make your soil resemble the rich, black, well-drained soils of other areas of the country. That is not easy because the average Utah topsoil contains less than 1 percent organic matter. To make matters

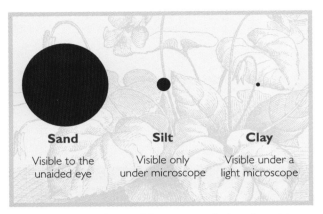

Sand	Silt	Clay
Visible to the unaided eye	Visible only under microscope	Visible under a light microscope

Soil texture is made up of three types of mineral particles: sand, silt, and clay.

worse, most new landscapes are planted in sterile, poor quality subsoil.

Soil Texture

To improve your soil, you must know its content. A soil's mineral matter is its weathered rock. Its texture refers to the size of its mineral particles, and its structure is the arrangement of those particles. The texture and structure affect the space between soil particles, known as the pore space. The pore space is important because it conveys water, nutrients, and air to the roots and provides space for them to grow.

The soil texture is made up of three types of mineral particles: sand, silt, and clay. Understanding what each does, you can compensate for and improve upon the particles to keep your garden growing well.

Soil particles range in size from gravel to fine particles. The proportion of the various particles determines the texture and feel of the soil.

Soil Types

The original soil at Temple Square was good agricultural soil washed down from City Creek Canyon, but the area has undergone many changes since the pioneers arrived. Among those changes are construction projects, starting with the Bowery and culminating most recently with the Conference Center. These projects have not always been kind to the soil, just as construction takes its toll on residential soils.

Sandy soil warms up early in the spring, provides good drainage, and resists compaction. It is easy to work because it does not become sticky or hard, but it does not hold water or nutrients well. To easily determine whether you have sandy soil, water your garden and then turn over a shovel full of soil. Take a handful of the moist soil and squeeze it together. If it doesn't stick together well and form a ball, you probably have sandy soil.

Clay soil is heavy because it retains moisture and repels air. It typically does not drain well. Because it has little oxygen available to plant roots, plants grow poorly. This is particularly true of annuals that don't have aggressive root systems.

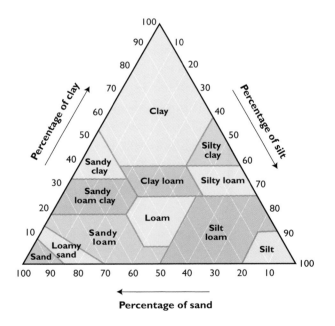

The relative amounts of sand, silt, and clay determine the type of soil in your garden. Soil scientists use a soil textural triangle to categorize soils.

To find out if you have clay, turn over a shovel full of soil. Then pick up a handful of moist soil and squeeze it together. If it forms a sticky ball that does not easily come apart, you have clay soil.

Loam soils contain nearly equal proportions of sand, silt, and clay. These soil components provide a good balance between holding moisture and nutrients in the ground, where the roots need it, and allowing oxygen to reach the roots. When you form a ball with moist loam, it will crumble without being excessively sticky.

A good soil holds sufficient water, nutrients, and oxygen for plant roots, and it provides adequate support to hold plants upright. Poor soils will not grow good plants. If your garden soil is lacking, you need to amend it to improve its quality.

Soil Testing

A soil test analyzes the chemical and other properties of your soil. By learning about your soil's content, you can manage it better and make your garden more attractive and more productive. A soil test will also help you decide which plants will grow well in your soil.

Utah State University Extension recommends a routine test for general sampling. The routine test measures soil pH (acidity or alkalinity), salinity (salt level), lime, texture class, and plant-available phosphorus and potassium. Resulting interpretations and recommendations are based on the test results and on the site background you provide with the sample.

The Utah State University Analytical Laboratory can also test for other elements. Other states throughout the country have similar services through the land grant system. For further information, contact your local county extension agent or the USU Analytical Labs at its web address: www.psb.usu.edu/tal/soil.science/usual.

Soil tests give you a good starting point to determine your soil's quality. A soil test is recommended every three to five years for home gardeners. As soil management intensifies, so should the frequency of soil testing. Highly productive landscapes that undergo frequent fertilizer, manure, or soil amendments should be tested often to monitor changing soil conditions and to prevent a buildup of excess levels of nutrients and salts.

Geraniums and heliotrope add beauty to the garden located north of the Beehive House.

Soil tests indicate whether plant nutrients are deficient and, if so, what amounts are needed for optimum growth. Soil testing is also a useful diagnostic tool to identify problems related to excessive levels of nutrients and salts, high pH, low organic matter, and poor drainage. Keep records of soil tests and fertilizer applications, and watch for resulting plant response.

pH Balance

The pH scale measures the level of acidity or alkalinity in soil. Various types of plants will grow with different pH levels, but a neutral level of pH is usually best because it allows plants to get the nutrients they need. It is important to know the pH level of your soil so you can either amend your soil or choose plants that will do well in your existing soil.

The pH scale runs from 1–14. Acid, or "sour," soil runs from 0–7; alkaline, or "sweet," soil runs from 7–14. Soil with a pH of 7 is considered neutral.

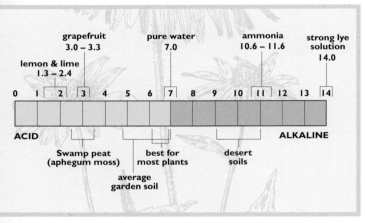

The pH scale measures the level of acidity or alkalinity in soil.

Soil Problems

In some areas of the world, topsoil is forty feet deep. On Temple Square, many of the beds are located above parking garages or other structures and are technically considered rooftop gardens, with depths ranging from four inches to three feet. Plants in rooftop gardens or in shallow home gardens do not have root systems that are as deep as those of plants grown in deeper soils. As a result, they offer less plant support.

Soil texture can also pose problems. A soil made of different textures may create barriers to plant roots, water flow, and air penetration. Root, water, and oxygen penetration changes if soil layers are composed of distinctly different textures. Sand or gravel layers stop normal downward water movement and root penetration. Water will not drain freely from a clay layer into sand or gravel until the clay becomes saturated. Waterlogged soil creates an interface between the plant and its roots, causing the roots to die from poor aeration.

One reason the beds at Temple Square grow plants so well is that these common soil problems are addressed and eliminated as much as possible

Water will not drain freely from a clay layer of soil into sand or gravel until the clay becomes saturated.

before planting. Occasionally, however, an existing planting bed may need to be amended to correct a soil problem. In one instance, the plants in a particular garden on the Church Office Building block were not thriving. Previously the bed had been torn up during construction and refilled with road base and construction dirt. The soil was compacted with no drainage. The gardener responsible for the planting bed decided to amend the soil to allow for better drainage of the entire bed. This

proved to be the cure, and that particular planting bed is now a beautiful, thriving perennial garden.

Dense hardpan layers of soil are impermeable to water and air drainage. Moisture accumulates above the hardpan but cannot soak through it. This layer must be shattered or perforated before plants can grow well.

In all Temple Square gardens, Utelite is used to improve the soil. If the soil is extremely poor, a combination of peat moss and Utelite is added. As you remodel and improve your planting beds, always try to increase the effective root depth for your plants. The better the plant roots grow, the better the plant top grows.

ORGANIC MATTER

As mentioned, an average soil has 5 percent organic matter. This humus, nutrient-rich component improves all kinds of soil as it alters soil structure. Adding organic matter is the easiest and best way to improve your soil.

Many types of organic matter can be added to soil to help create the type of texture you want. If you have sandy soil, you can add almost any organic matter, including peat moss, to help regulate soil moisture. If you have clay soil, you can add coarse organic matter like sawdust to help lighten the soil and make it easier for roots to establish themselves. Don't mix peat moss and clay. Both are like sponges, and the resulting mix holds too much water.

Mulch. Mulch covers the soil to control weeds, conserve moisture, and insulate against extreme temperatures. Mulch also breaks down and improves soil structure, and it enhances garden appearance. Mulches can be organic or inorganic materials, but landscape mulches are generally organic.

Common organic mulches are bark, sawdust, pine needles, grass clippings, shredded leaves, shredded newspaper, and wood chips. You can also buy commercial mixtures and composts (decomposed organic material). Inorganic mulches include gravel, plastic or woven landscape fabrics, sand, and stone. Landscape fabrics are especially useful in controlling weeds.

Mulches are added in the fall to insulate plants against cold temperatures. This insulation helps prevent winter desiccation and frost heaving, which can force plants out of the ground as a result of the alternate freezing and thawing. If you live in an area with cold winters, wait until the ground freezes and then spread two to three inches of light mulch over your beds. Winter mulch is not put on to keep the soil from freezing but to keep it from thawing. This helps plants go dormant and remain dormant so that they don't die when temperatures fluctuate.

In the spring after the soil has warmed up, clear all weeds from your garden before mulching again. Then spread two to three inches of mulch over the soil without covering the crowns of the plants. Too much mulch next to plant stems can lead to problems with pests or disease.

Compost. Composting is a natural process by which organic material decomposes into humus. It is a great way to recycle organic waste from the garden and kitchen. Compost is an excellent mulch. During the growing season, 30 percent of landfill waste is potential compost. Composting at home helps ease landfill problems and creates humus that can increase soil fertility, water holding capacity, and drainage.

Composting methods range from piling up leftover organic materials and waste so they can decompose over time (thirty to ninety days), to sophisticated composting systems that mechanically turn and water the compost.

Microorganisms, earthworms, small insects, and other soil organisms decompose organic matter as they use it for food. Decomposition requires carbon, nitrogen, water, oxygen, and heat. When these occur in the right ratios, decomposition produces heat that speeds the process and kills most weed seeds and harmful pathogens.

Carbon is the principal component of all organic matter. A material must have a proper ratio of carbon to nitrogen, termed "C:N ratio," to compost properly. The most efficient ratio for composting is fifteen to thirty parts carbon (or compost) per one part nitrogen. If the ratio is too high or low, the composting process is slowed.

If oxygen is lacking, the compost decomposes anaerobically (without oxygen). The decaying process is slow and causes foul odors. You can supply adequate oxygen by frequently turning your compost.

NUTRIENTS

All garden soils are combinations of organic and mineral components. Plants use the nutrients in these components to grow. Soil nutrients become available for plant growth as living soil organisms break down organic matter and release nutrients. They also become available through natural mineral degradation as the sun, wind, frost, and rain make mineral elements available.

Most garden soils are relatively high in nutrients when compared to a plant's requirements. Unfortunately, much of this potential supply is in a form plants cannot use, or it is in a form that is not supplied quickly enough to produce satisfactory plant growth. Using fertilizers helps make up for this deficiency.

Plant growth depends upon a favorable combination of light, mechanical support, heat, air, water, and nutrients. If any of these factors is out of balance with the others, plant growth is reduced. This principle of limiting factors is stated this way: "The level of plant growth can be no

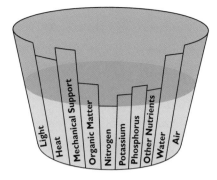

Each slat of the bucket above represents an element or nutrient essential for plant growth. The amount of water in the bucket represents maximum plant growth, which is limited by the shortest slat (in this case, nitrogen). When the level of nitrogen increases, plant growth will likewise increase. The plant can grow only as much as allowed by available nutrients.

greater than is allowed by the most limiting essential growth factor."

Essential Elements

Plants require seventeen elements for proper growth. Although many commercial products claim that they contain other needed materials, plants use only seventeen elements to manufacture their food.

Some so-called experts would have you believe

ESSENTIAL ELEMENTS AND THEIR SOURCES			
MACRONUTRIENTS		**MICRONUTRIENTS**	
Mostly from Air and Water	From Soil	From Soil	
Carbon (C)	Nitrogen (N)	Iron (Fe)	Copper (Cu)
Hydrogen (H)	Phosphorus (P)	Manganese (Mn)	Zinc (Z)
Oxygen (O)	Potassium (K)	Boron (B)	Chlorine (Cl)
	Calcium (Ca)	Cobalt (Co)	
	Sulfur (S)	Molybdenum (Mo)	
	Magnesium (Mg)		

Plants use seventeen macronutrients and micronutrients to manufacture their food.

that what you put on your plants is what makes them grow, but that is not true. Approximately 97 percent of fresh plant tissue is made up of carbon, oxygen, and hydrogen. Plants get most of their carbon and oxygen directly from the air, while hydrogen comes from the water in the soil. These sources supply the bulk of plant tissue, the remainder of which—between 0.5 and 6 percent—comes from the soil.

Except in cases of drought, cold weather, poor drainage, and disease, plant growth is not generally reduced by inadequate carbon, oxygen, and hydrogen. Growth, however, is retarded if the soil lacks the other nutrients altogether, if they become available too slowly, or if they are not adequately balanced in the soil.

All other essential plant elements come from the soil except nitrogen derived from nitrogen-fixing bacteria. The absence of these other essential elements is likely to limit plant development. That's why we use fertilizers, which are designed to amend the soil with the fourteen other needed elements.

Essential nutrients are divided into two categories: macronutrients and micronutrients. This classification is based only on the relative amounts plants use and does not imply their relative importance. All are essential.

The six elements plants use in relatively large quantities are nitrogen, phosphorus, potassium, calcium, magnesium, and sulfur. These are designated as macronutrients. Of these elements, plants absorb nitrogen in the greatest quantity.

Nitrogen. Nitrogen promotes rapid growth of aboveground leafy tissue and gives plants a healthy deep-green color. Nitrogen is used in young plant tissues as protein. If available nitrogen does not meet a plant's needs, new shoots will use the protein at the expense of the older leaves, causing a characteristic general yellowing of mature leaves in nitrogen-deficient plants.

Nitrogen, supplied through fertilizers, is the

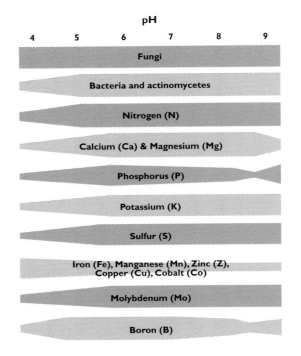

To maintain a good pH, a proper balance of nutrients must be found in the soil. For example, if the soil lacks nitrogen (N), the soil pH will be lower.

element that Temple Square gardeners add most frequently. Nitrogen for plant growth also comes from the atmosphere, soil, organic or mineral matter in the soil, and mineral fraction. Unlike many other soil elements, nitrogen is transient in the soil. It is taken up by plant roots and used to make plant protein, leached through the soil by irrigation, converted to nitrogen gas by bacteria and lost to the atmosphere, trapped on clay particles in the soil, or decomposed and used by soil microorganisms. Because it disappears from the soil quickly, nitrogen must be supplied as needed. If you apply dry nitrogen fertilizers, use them every four to six weeks in your lawn and flower bed areas. You can apply diluted liquid fertilizers more frequently.

Phosphorus. Phosphorus, or phosphate, is essential to all phases of plant growth, especially in promoting flower and fruit growth. Visible signs of inadequate phosphorus appear first in the lower, older leaves. Symptoms include a lack of chlorophyll and a color change in the leaves—changing to dark green or purple.

Unlike nitrogen, phosphorus does not move in the soil or convert to a gas. When phosphorus fertilizer is applied to the soil, it stays right where it is applied. This element is rapidly converted into a form that is unavailable to plants, so it is usually applied once each season. Phosphorus is least available in cool weather, so adding it is especially important during early spring plantings.

Because phosphorus is often contained in fertilizer blends and animal manures, it can build up to excessive amounts in the soil. Do not add phosphorus every time you fertilize, and check levels every few years by getting a soil test. By combining with other plant nutrients, excess phosphorus turns them into unavailable compounds.

Potassium. Potassium, also called potash, is used in large amounts by plants. Potassium levels in Utah soils are high. Generally, you need to add little or no potassium to your garden unless you are using artificial or highly amended soilless mixes.

Potassium is essential to plants. It increases their disease resistance, helps them overcome adverse weather or soil conditions, and contributes to their overall vigor. Under normal growing conditions, many plants use three to four times as much potassium and nitrogen as they do phosphorus.

These three elements—nitrogen, phosphorus, and potassium—are the main ingredients of commercial fertilizers. The letters N for nitrogen, P for phosphorus, and K for potassium appear on fertilizer bags and containers with a corresponding number to identify the amount of each ingredient.

The next three macronutrients—**calcium, magnesium,** and **sulfur**—are not likely to be in short supply in your garden in Utah. Calcium levels, in fact, are excessive in Utah soils. Adding calcium in the form of lime, dolomite, or gypsum is unnecessary and even harmful to Utah soils.

Snapdragon, vinca, lobelia, African daisy, and petunia produce a beautiful outdoor bouquet.

Liming raises the soil pH, and the pH of our soils is already too high. Sulfur occurs naturally in decomposing organic matter. Plants also receive sulfur from the atmosphere in industrial areas, in the form of sulfur dioxide.

Plants use the other nutrient elements—iron, manganese, copper, zinc, boron, molybdenum, chlorine, and cobalt—in such small amounts that they are called micronutrients. But this designation does not mean they are less essential than the macronutrients.

Fortunately, Utah gardeners needn't worry about micronutrients. Nature supplies most of these. Add them only when deficiency symptoms or soil tests show a need. Many commercial fertilizers contain micronutrients as part of their formulations. These products are excellent for hanging baskets or other container plantings.

Iron chlorosis is a common plant disorder that affects many plants grown on Temple Square. It is usually the only micronutrient problem Utah gardeners have to deal with. But it is not caused by a lack of iron, which is usually plentiful in Utah soils. The problem is that Utah's alkaline soils are high in calcium, which combines with iron and makes it unavailable to plants. Overwatering (which kills absorbing roots) and excessive phosphorus from fertilizer (which combines with iron) also make iron unavailable to plants.

Many plants do not have the ability to absorb enough iron in alkaline soils. Silver maple, red maple, pin oak, blueberries, cranberries, magnolias, azaleas, and rhododendrons struggle in alkaline soils. Areas on Temple Square that are home to these trees and plants have been amended with peat moss and other acidic amendments. Selecting iron-efficient plants and controlling water are the best ways to prevent iron chlorosis problems.

Iron chlorosis symptoms often show up in July and August after available iron is depleted around plant roots. Newer leaves turn yellow while leaf veins remain dark green. Severe iron chlorosis turns leaves completely yellow, after which they scorch and turn brown. Iron does not move inside plants after they use it, so newer leaves are affected first.

SOIL TYPE AND PLANT NUTRIENTS

Soil texture dramatically affects the availability of plant nutrients. Sand holds few nutrients, and fertilizer washes readily through sand. Clay soils attract nutrients and hold them for a longer time. Amending sand or clay soils with organic matter improves their nutrient-holding capacity. Soil pH also affects the ability of plants to absorb nutrients.

Fertilizers

Plants grow best if nutrients are available at the time and in the amounts they need them. Develop a regular, recommended fertilization schedule rather than waiting until your plants begin to suffer.

Fertilizer bags and containers list three letters. As mentioned above, these letters refer to nitrogen (N), phosphorus (P), and potassium (K). A label of 10–10–10 means that the fertilizer contains 10 percent nitrogen, 10 percent phosphorus compounds, and 10 percent potassium compounds. The remaining 70 percent is composed of other chemicals or mixing agents that allow the fertilizer to be spread evenly on the soil.

Complete fertilizers contain the three primary nutrients in varying percentages but may not contain all the nutrients your plants need. In addition, complete fertilizers may cause a phosphorous buildup. Always read the instructions carefully and apply as recommended. If you live outside Utah, get local information on what nutrients your plants need. Call your local county extension agency.

Types of Fertilizers

Fertilizers come in many forms, including dry fertilizer, time-release fertilizer, foliar fertilizer, liquid fertilizer, special-purpose fertilizer, and natural organic fertilizer.

Dry Fertilizer
- Comes in granules, powders, or pellets.
- Dissolves over time.
- Is scattered or worked into the soil before planting.

Time-Release Fertilizer
- Is composed of dry or encased granules that last three–fourteen months.
- Releases nutrients over time under specific conditions.
- Eliminates the need for frequent feeding.

Foliar Fertilizer

- Is sprayed on plant leaves.
- Allows leaves to absorb nutrients directly and immediately.
- May damage leaves when used in hot weather.

Liquid Fertilizer

- Composed of soluble granules mixed with water.
- Can be applied to leaves or soil during watering.
- Is used with drip irrigation systems.
- Provides immediate nutrients to leaves and roots.

Special-Purpose Fertilizer

- Contains specific nutrient blends.
- Created for the needs of particular plants.

Natural Organic Fertilizer

- Created from plant or animal residues such as manure, bonemeal, or fish emulsion.
- Occurs naturally in rock products.
- Releases nutrients slowly.
- Has low nutrient content.

Excess Fertilizer

Fertilizers are salts. When salt is applied to soil, water moves toward it. If tender plant roots are close to salt or fertilizer, water is drawn from these roots to dilute the salts. As water is drawn from the roots, plant cells dehydrate and burn.

Never apply excessive amounts of fertilizer, and make sure adequate moisture is available after your application. Fertilizers do not burn or damage plants if they are applied at the right time, rate, and location (not too close to plant roots).

WATER AND IRRIGATION

Most of Utah needs water if it is ever to "blossom as the rose" (Isaiah 35:1). During the early years on Temple Square, the long rows of elms between the Tabernacle and the Salt Lake Temple were sustained by buckets of water dipped into City Creek and hand carried to the trees. City Creek, which has since been diverted underground, ran through Temple Square back then. Today an archway on the lower west wall of Temple Square marks the approximate location of the creek.

Large amounts of water are needed to produce showy flower beds and to keep other plants flourishing. For each pound of dry matter a plant produces, it uses from three hundred to seven hundred pounds of water. If water is not supplied on demand, plant growth will be restricted. Annual precipitation in Salt Lake City is twelve to sixteen inches per year, and much of that occurs when annual plants are not able to utilize it. Crops may require thirty to forty inches of precipitation per year during the growing season, so properly applied irrigation is a vital concern to the growth of healthy, vigorous plants.

Landscapes use water in two ways. The first is evaporation from the soil surface. The rate of

An archway in the fence north of the west entrance to Temple Square marks the approximate location of City Creek before it was diverted underground.

evaporation varies depending on sunlight intensity, vegetation cover, temperature, wind, and relative humidity. Mulches can reduce evaporation losses.

The second category of water use is transpiration, which is the movement of water through a plant. When the stomata (small structures on the back of the leaves that regulate gas and moisture exchange) are open, water is pulled through the plant by transpiration and lost from the leaves through evaporation. This accounts for about 90 percent of the water that enters the plant through the roots. The other 10 percent is used in plant tissues and in chemical reactions such as photosynthesis, during which water supplies oxygen and hydrogen in the manufacturing of sugars.

Transpiration also moves minerals, sugars, hormones, and other chemicals through the plant. It maintains turgor pressure and cools the plant through evaporation. The amount of water lost from the plant depends on the same environmental factors that affect evaporation.

Soils work as reservoirs, supplying plants with water held from precipitation or irrigation. Most landscapes require that soil moisture be recharged in order to provide for good plant growth. However, much of the water applied to the soil is not available to or utilized by plants. When water soaks into the soil, air is displaced and pores are filled with water. Continued watering causes further downward movement and air replacement. When all soil pores are filled, the soil is saturated, holding as much water as it can. When the water supply stops, some water still moves downward out of the larger pores and is replaced by air. The soil is then at "field capacity." The smaller pores are still filled with water, creating a reservoir from which plants can absorb water.

As the soil dries out, plants suffer from lack of soil moisture. During the daytime, they wilt, especially if it's windy or hot. They temporarily recover at night, but unless they receive water they will reach a permanent wilting point and die. Finer soils store more water than coarse, textured ones. Sandy soils require more frequent irrigation but require smaller amounts of water than loamy or clay soils. Organic matter helps increase the moisture-holding capacity of a soil.

Plants grow best if levels of soil moisture are consistent, but some plants can tolerate extreme levels better than others. Willows and poplars can survive wet soils, while junipers are frequently killed by overwatering. For best growth and fewer problems, group plants according to water needs.

In some soils and plantings, tremendous amounts of water are wasted because of surface runoff. This is caused by excessive slope, rapid application rate, or the inability of the soil to absorb the water. Compacted or crusted soils, soils with high clay content, soils with impermeable layers such as thatch on a lawn, and soils that lack a vegetative cover all slow or prohibit infiltration.

Major water loss also occurs through percolation. This downward movement of excessive amounts of water wastes this resource and depletes the soil of nutrients. Save water by giving soil and plants only as much as they need.

IRRIGATION

Your watering schedule depends on many variables, including sun, wind, humidity, and temperature. Always water your landscape thoroughly; then let the soil dry out before watering again. Overwatering causes plants to rot.

Water should penetrate at least eight inches into the soil to reach plant roots. Use a probe to check water penetration. The best time of day to water is in the early morning. This gives leaves a chance to dry out during the day.

In the Salt Lake area, salts may play an important role in irrigation scheduling. Salts come from

A typical shade garden on Temple Square features coleus, tuberous begonia, Boston fern, and fibrous begonia.

Furrow irrigation commonly used by the pioneers is recreated at the Brigham Young Historic Park.

Drip irrigation is typically the most efficient way to water your garden.

naturally occurring compounds or chemical salts in fertilizers. As salt concentrations increase, plants have more difficulty absorbing soil moisture. Excess salt prevents healthy plant growth and often burns plant leaves. Frequent irrigation dilutes and leaches salts from soil that drains well, but added water can be detrimental to poorly drained soils.

Landscape can be watered in many ways. Experiment to see which method, or combination of methods, works best for your garden. Common methods include:

Furrow irrigation. Originally, Temple Square gardens, as well as gardens throughout the Salt Lake Valley, were watered through furrow irrigation. This method works well for vegetable gardens and orchards but not for most landscapes, which are not planted in long, straight rows. A representation of this method has been recreated in the Brigham Young Historic Park located east of the Church Office Building.

Sprinklers. Underground sprinkler systems are effective, especially for large landscapes. Install a timer on your sprinkling system to make sure your garden has the water it needs when it needs it. Most gardens on Temple Square are sprinkler irrigated on a timed schedule and are adjusted according to weather conditions. Watering with a sprinkler on a hose is also effective, but it takes more time and thought.

Drip systems. Drip irrigation, when designed and installed correctly, is typically the most efficient method because water drips directly from a hose to where it is needed. Use a timer to regulate the water, and check to make sure that the holes in the system do not become clogged.

Hand watering. Unless you have a small garden, choose another method. Hand watering is adequate for newly transplanted beds, containers, and hanging baskets. Remember that these may need to be watered several times each day during the summer.

WEEDS

Weeds compete with your plants for water, nutrients, and light. Worse, they don't look good! Winning the war against weeds is hard work. But with consistent effort and right methods, you can win the war. One of the best weapons in your war on weeds is to learn their life cycle.

Common Weed Life Cycles

Weeds can be placed into five groups: annual grasses, annual broadleaf plants, perennial grasses, perennial broadleaf plants, and woody plants.

Summer annuals grow from seeds that sprout in the spring and mature and reproduce before dying in the winter. Common summer annuals are barnyard grass, puncture vine, Russian thistle, and pigweed. Winter annuals germinate in the fall or winter and flower, produce seed, and die in the spring. Common winter annuals are bluegrass, chickweed, mustard, and downy brome (or Junegrass).

Biennial weeds require two years to complete their life cycles. These plants usually grow vegetatively (without flowering) the first year. In the second year they flower, produce seed, and die. Common biennial weeds are musk thistle, mullein, and hound's-tongue.

Perennials live three years or longer. These plants flower and set seed without dying. Most die back in the winter but resume growth in the spring. Common perennials are quack grass, bindweed (morning glory), dandelion, and plantain.

Woody plants live for more than three years. Unlike the other categories, these plants do not die back. Most treatments for woody plants require that their bark be cut so that herbicide can be absorbed into the plants.

Weed Control

Weeds are the most serious, time-consuming, and expensive problem associated with ornamental plants. The earth was cursed to bring forth thistles and weeds, and that happens in the Temple Square gardens just as it does in your garden. For most weeds, prevention, rather than warfare, is the best control.

Let flowers and plants help your garden by forming a "plant canopy" over your beds. Where your plants flourish, weeds are not nearly as likely to grow.

Nature never tolerates bare ground. You can till your garden until it is free of weeds, but if you water it and wait three weeks, it will be covered with thousands of weeds. One successful approach to weed control is to keep your garden growing. Let your flowers and plants help you by keeping a "plant canopy" over your beds. Where your plants flourish, weeds are not nearly as likely to grow.

Go after weeds when they're small. A few strokes with a sharp gliding hoe can remove many weeds. If you let weeds get three feet tall, you may never get them out. The most success we have in weed control is to prevent weeds from reproducing, so never let weeds go to seed in your garden. If you let weeds go to seed, you can count on those seeds producing weeds for up to twenty-five more years. Field bindweed can stay dormant for about fifty years!

Prevention

Watch what you bring into your garden. Gardeners introduce many problems with topsoil, manure, and other soil amendments. Keep out anything that is suspect. Use soil amendments that are fully composted to kill pests, and avoid bringing in soil that could be full of weed seeds. Also, make sure no weeds are growing in the soil of perennial and annual plants that you bring to your garden. If so, gently scrape off the top layer of the soil and throw it away.

Many gardeners believe they can control all their weed problems using herbicides. While these products are useful in some situations, the best tools for weeding are hands, hoes, and diggers. As a general rule, we keep use of herbicides to a minimum at Temple Square, mainly using them to target specific problem weeds. This is particularly true of our flower beds. Because we grow so many kinds of flowers and change our beds frequently, we must avoid potential herbicide buildup in the soil.

Once the weeds are out of the beds, a good weed-free mulch is an excellent weapon. Several inches of mulch will prevent most annual weeds from germinating. Unfortunately, mulch does not control deep-rooted perennial weeds.

Using chemical controls requires a thorough familiarity with weeds, desirable plants, and the herbicides you intend to use. Follow label directions and apply herbicides at the correct time to achieve good control.

TARGET WEED GROUPS

Broadleaf weeds. Several post-emergent herbicides applied after weed seedlings appear selectively control annual, biennial, and perennial broadleaf weeds. These herbicides are used alone or in combinations. Spring and fall applications give satisfactory control and reduce the damage to desirable plants. Spot treatments are most effective for scattered weeds. Broadleaf weed killer (which contains 2, 4-D) is best used for weed control in lawns rather than in gardens because it can move through the soil or drift as a gas and kill desirable plants.

For general annual weed infestations, treat with pre-emergent herbicides. Spot treat with post-emergent herbicides for local infestations.

Few herbicides are safe on newly seeded turf and ornamentals. Some pre-emergent herbicides adversely affect grass germination later in the season, and some grasses are prone to herbicide injury. Check labels for precautions.

Perennial grass weeds are hard to control in turf. No herbicides can control these weeds without damaging cool-season turf, though some selectively control them in warm-season turf. Soil fumigants and nonselective herbicides also kill desirable grasses.

Field bindweed. Controlling field bindweed is one of the toughest challenges we face in the Temple Square gardens. This weed seems to defy control and can explode from a small patch into a total infestation.

Bindweed has several aliases, including wild morning glory, creeping jenny, European bindweed, and a whole host of other names not suitable for publication in this book. *Convolvulus arvensis,* its scientific name, is native to Europe and likely came to Utah in contaminated crop seed.

Bindweed has a prodigious ability to reproduce. Like the morning glory plant it resembles, bindweed produces a new crop of one-inch funnel-shaped flowers each day; each flower then produces four seeds each day. These seeds have an exceptional survival ability, remaining viable for up to fifty years.

Bindweed can best be attacked in early summer when in full bloom or when fall arrives. Glyphosate, commonly known as Roundup, is probably the easiest and safest product. It is non-selective and affects any plant it touches. To keep it off desirable plants, cut the bottom off an old milk jug or plastic soda bottle. Insert your spray wand into the opening on the top. Set the jug over the top of the plant, pulling the plant's vines into the jug, and spray. This keeps the overspray from hitting other plants. Leaving the jug over the plant forces the weed to absorb the herbicide.

Bindweed control in established plantings is difficult. Use spray bottles, sponges, or paint brushes to apply herbicide to the weed without getting it on desirable plants. Apply herbicide to bindweed growing among desirable plants by using a cotton glove over a rubber glove. Dip the glove into weed killer and wipe it onto the leaves.

Glyphosate does not carry over into the soil, but it will translocate into bindweed's extensive root and rhizome system. If you don't kill the underground part of the plant, your control will be inconsistent and temporary.

In the fall, about the time of the first frost, spray plants with glyphosate or a mixture of glyphosate and a lawn weed killer containing 2,4-D. Because plants are moving their nutrients from leaves to roots in the fall, herbicides sprayed on leaves will find their way to the roots. Do not use 2, 4-D in beds that have desirable plants.

All herbicide treatments work best when weeds are actively growing, but 2,4-D should not be used during the heat of the summer or near trees or shrubs because it damages desirable plants. Sprays do not work well on plants that are under stress from drought or other conditions. Water and fertilize them well for several weeks before spraying. Spray plants off with water to remove dust, which deactivates herbicides. After treating, do not water the sprayed areas for six to eight hours, and do not

Controlling field bindweed is one of the toughest challenges gardeners face on Temple Square.

spray if rain is expected. The herbicide must remain on the leaves until it is absorbed.

Carefully mix and use all herbicides according to label directions. Spray weeds so that the foliage is thoroughly wet, but avoid using excessive amounts of herbicide. Excessive chemicals burn off weed tops, preventing herbicides from being translocated to plant roots.

Despite your best efforts, bindweed often comes back with a vengeance. Keep up the battle year after year, and you may win the war.

Chapter 3

Planning a Garden

Thomas Hobbs sums up the goal of the gardener in his book *Shocking Beauty:* "The ultimate compliment to a great garden [and gardener] is when a visitor is reduced to hobbling—there is so much to see and ask about, it is impossible to take a normal step" (Vancouver, British Columbia: Raincoast, 1999, vi).

Creating a successful garden space is a matter of planning. Good planning saves both time and money and results in a garden you can be proud of. But good planning requires knowledge.

The first step to creating a beautiful, healthy garden is to assess the area where the garden will be located. You need to know the cold hardiness and heat zone of the region in which you live. You need to determine your soil type, the average rainfall and freeze-thaw patterns of your area, the sun and shade patterns in your garden space, and how often and how severely the winds blow. Consider all possible problems. Planning a garden requires careful thought because conditions interact and combine to determine how successful your garden will be.

SOIL PREPARATION

Soil preparation is one of the most important factors in planning a garden and is discussed in detail in chapter 2, "Gardening Basics." After you determine your soil type, amend it with whatever it needs to give your plants optimal growing conditions. As noted in chapter 2, it is usually better to work with existing soil than to bring in soil from another location that may contain weeds and diseases.

Very little high-grade topsoil is available in urban areas of Utah. In most cases, incorporating organic matter or Utelite into existing soil will provide a much better environment with which to work. Utelite's porous texture helps break up clay soil and improve drainage so that roots can get enough oxygen for healthy root growth. This is important because many homeowners overwater their plants. Plants need oxygen as much as they need water. The benefits of Utelite far outweigh the effort needed to incorporate it into your soil.

If your garden site is covered with weeds, you will need to get rid of them. The time spent to rid

A wall-mounted flower box along the Center mall overflows with yellow ranunculus, Iceland poppies, and basket-of-gold in a sea of aubrieta and arabis.

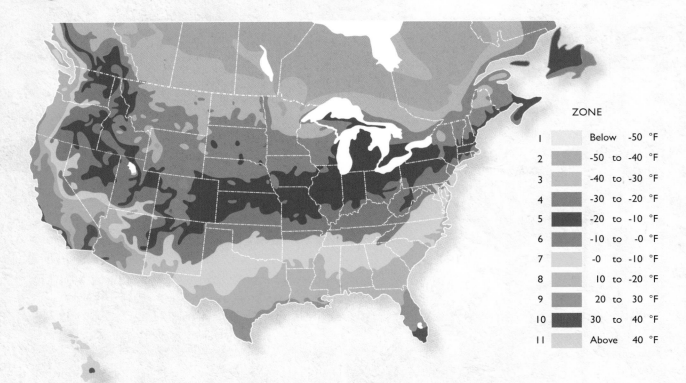

ZONE		
1	Below	-50 °F
2	-50 to	-40 °F
3	-40 to	-30 °F
4	-30 to	-20 °F
5	-20 to	-10 °F
6	-10 to	-0 °F
7	-0 to	-10 °F
8	10 to	-20 °F
9	20 to	30 °F
10	30 to	40 °F
11	Above	40 °F

The USDA Plant Hardiness Zone Map identifies eleven zones determined by average minimum temperatures that can be expected each year in the United States. The detail map of Utah (below), which is from the 1990 U.S. National Arboretum version of the USDA Plant Hardiness Zone Map, provides greater detail by subdividing each zone into light- and dark-colored sections that represent cooler and warmer areas within that zone.

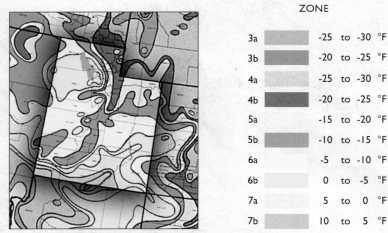

Agricultural Research Service, USDA

ZONE		
3a	-25 to	-30 °F
3b	-20 to	-25 °F
4a	-25 to	-30 °F
4b	-20 to	-25 °F
5a	-15 to	-20 °F
5b	-10 to	-15 °F
6a	-5 to	-10 °F
6b	0 to	-5 °F
7a	5 to	0 °F
7b	10 to	5 °F

USDA Plant Hardiness Zone Map

your garden space of weeds before you plant will save many hours of weeding later. Remember, weed seeds can survive twenty years or more in your soil.

WATER REQUIREMENTS

The annual precipitation in Utah is relatively low. In Utah's desert climate, people must rely on water stored from winter snowfall to carry them through the rest of the year. When winter snowfall is lower than average, however, summer water supplies can become limited. This makes water conservation an important factor in selecting plants. Minimizing the amount of water-loving plants and using drought-tolerant plants helps decrease water consumption.

Knowing when and how often to water plants is essential. The best time to water is early morning when the temperature and evaporation rate are at their lowest. Most plants need more water while becoming established but need only occasional watering afterward. A good practice is less frequent, deep watering so that roots will grow deeper and be better able to endure hot temperatures.

Learning to recognize signs of water stress in plants will help you determine how often you need to water. Parched lawns start to show signs of water stress when they turn a dull grayish green and footprints remain depressed and visible. Remember, however, that a dry soil surface does not necessarily mean it is time to water. For flower beds, dig down four to five inches to see if the soil is moist where the roots are growing. Sometimes aerating the ground to improve water circulation can be more important than additional watering. As mentioned in chapters 2 and 7, mulching helps soil retain moisture.

Soil type also determines water needs. Sandy soil drains quickly and requires more water. To increase water retention, add organic material. Clay soil drains slowly and should be amended with Utelite or organic material to prevent runoff and to allow deep water penetration.

LIGHT REQUIREMENTS

Sun and shade patterns affect plant growth. Before you purchase any plants, do a sun and shade study to record the movements of shade patterns throughout the day. Standing in the same location, take pictures of a specific garden area every hour throughout the day. You will be amazed at the changing sun and shade patterns revealed by your photographs, which will help you determine which areas have deep shade, filtered shade, half shade, or full shade. This information will enable you to buy the right plant for the right location. The following chart gives a general definition of the typical sun-shade designations for plants.

Many plants need full sun in order to thrive.

A shade garden behind the Beehive House features Boston fern, browallia, and impatiens.

Full sun	6–8 hours of full sun each day
Partial sun	4–6 hours of full sun each day
Partial shade	4–6 hours of filtered sun each day
Full shade	Less than 4 hours of sun each day
Deep shade	No sun

While full sun is defined as six to eight hours of direct sunlight each day, the intensity of sunlight varies according to the time of day. Plants requiring full sun may flourish with only five hours of afternoon sun, while others may need more than six hours of sun, mostly in the morning.

Sun requirements in Utah differ than in other parts of the country. Plants that need full sun in other areas may need only partial sun in Utah because the sun and heat are so intense. Partial sun and partial shade are fairly interchangeable terms in specifying light requirements, but it is

wise to remember that areas of dry shade and moist shade can affect plants differently. Some plants adapt to their environment and will do well in a little more or less sun and shade than specified.

WIND CONDITIONS

Wind patterns can make or break a garden site very quickly. Wind dries out the moisture in the leaves of plants. It can also pull water from the surface of the soil, creating drought-like conditions. If wind is a problem in your garden space, address it in the planning stage. You can reduce wind in several ways. Plant a barrier of coniferous evergreen shrubs and trees, build a wall or fence, or place the flower beds by an existing building or structure.

MICROCLIMATES

Microclimates occur when the climatic conditions in a particular area differ from the surrounding climate. Varying wind exposure, temperature, sun exposure, and humidity may create different microclimates within the same yard. Microclimates are relatively small areas but can vary in size from the shady area beneath a tree to the garden surrounding a pond. Recognizing the microclimates in your garden can help you select plant materials for each location.

Microclimates in the gardens of Temple Square can be found in such areas as beneath the deodar trees in the Lion House tea garden. This area is a microclimate because the garden is surrounded on three sides by buildings and on the fourth side by a row of pine trees. These protect the tea garden area and help create an area warmer than a garden in an open space.

A more mild microclimate may allow you to push a plant's hardiness zone limit and experiment

Microclimates on the three blocks of Temple Square can be found in areas such as under the deodar cedars in the Lion House tea garden.

Wisteria vine, petunia, 'Victoria Blue' salvia, geraniums, and daylilies garnish the pergola south of the Relief Society Building.

Hot red salvia, 'Lemon Gem' marigold, silver artemisia, purple sweet alyssum, and bright pink geraniums provide a steady supply of color along the walkway to the Beehive House and the Lion House.

with plants that might typically be considered for warmer climates. You may lose a few plants, but you may also find a few plants that survive.

Each side of your house has its own unique microclimate zones and should be treated accordingly in planning your garden. Consider the following general guidelines for the microclimates created by your house. It is assumed that your house sits on an open, level site.

South side
- Receives the most sun exposure throughout the year.
- Is the warmest area in the winter.
- Warms up earlier in the spring.

East side
- Receives morning sun.
- Benefits from afternoon shade.
- Is a good location for plants that need half a day of sun and half a day of shade.

North side
- Receives mostly shade all day.
- Receives a small amount of sun morning and evening.
- Requires mostly all-day shade plants.

West side
- Receives direct afternoon sun exposure.
- Benefits from morning shade.

SPECIAL CONSIDERATIONS

Take particular note of problem areas in your garden. These could include a sloping area where water runoff creates difficulties, an area where cold air drains to the bottom of a hill and causes frost pockets, or an area where winter snow does not melt for long periods because of northeast exposure. Deer and other animals, even pets, can cause a great deal of damage if not managed properly with fences, barriers, and deer-resistant plants. Areas of high animal traffic should be planned for accordingly.

Because plants react differently at different altitude and humidity levels, note the altitude and amount of humidity in your proposed garden areas. For example, high mountain valleys may have a much shorter growth season than does the Salt Lake Valley.

Whether creating a new garden space or renovating an existing one, you can make your gardening experience more successful by addressing special considerations in the planning stage.

PLANNING FOR MAINTENANCE

Decide how many hours a week you want to spend taking care of your garden. The size of your garden makes this an important factor. A large area will obviously take longer to maintain than a small area. How you use your garden space will also determine the amount of time you will need.

The level of neatness you wish to maintain also determines the amount of time you will need for upkeep and should be considered in selecting plant types and varieties. Some plants have neat

Flower boxes, featuring coleus, impatiens, geranium, sweet potato vine, and sweet alyssum, adorn the wall of the center mall just west of the Salt Lake Temple.

and tidy growth habits, while others need help keeping an attractive appearance. Neatly trimmed edges of shrubs, for example, take more time to maintain than more natural edges.

SELECTING A STYLE

Now comes the fun part of the process, which is to choose a style or theme that fits you and your garden site. You may prefer a style that is artistic and symmetrical or naturalistic and asymmetrical. Gardens are usually designed in a formal, an informal, or a naturalistic style. The style of a garden is created primarily by the structure of the space, the types of plants selected, and the placement of the plants within that space. The style of a garden sets a mood that should complement its surroundings.

Choosing a theme is beneficial to garden design, not as a hard-and-fast rule but as a helpful guide. A theme will help you stay on track.

TEMPLE SQUARE GARDEN THEMES

Cottage style. The gardens around the Beehive House and the Lion House were designed to be in character with the architecture of the buildings. Cottage gardens are informal in style and feature a wide variety of colorful plants growing together.

Formal. Formal gardens are planted with strict

Tulips, pansies, sedums, aurinia, and arabis in a charming cottage style greet Lion House patrons and passersby.

symmetry and equally balanced plantings. Sheared hedges often line walkways and outline borders. The parterre gardens between the Church Administration Building and the Joseph Smith Memorial Building are laid out as formal gardens, although the flowers within the sharply defined borders are arranged informally.

Naturalistic. This style imitates nature as closely as possible. Native plants are used to make a setting that fits in with the natural surrounding area. Several types of natural plantings can be found at the Conference Center, where a meadow has been planted on the roof to reflect the Utah foothills. Native trees and shrubs can be found on the exterior ledges of the building, and a woodland theme is featured at the back of the building.

Formal clipped boxwood hedges outline this parterre garden bursting with tulips, wallflowers, and pansies.

'Lady in Red' salvia, amaranthus, four-o'clocks, fountain grass, and roses are arranged in this Temple Square bed to look as nature may have intended.

Drought-tolerant summer perennials show a naturalistic style west of the Conference Center.

A meadow planted on the roof of the Conference Center reflects the Utah foothills.

Chapter 4

Designing a Garden

We believe that the most beautiful way to create a garden is to design it as nature would design it within her own natural boundaries. As we look around this beautiful world, we notice that nature has her own style and never places vegetation in straight lines, concentric circles, checkerboards, or zipper patterns. And nature rarely spells words or forms images with vegetation. Such obvious patterns show that someone was in the garden taking too much control over nature's natural patterns, thus turning our eye to the earthly designer rather than toward the Creator.

Nature designs in explosions, sine curves, C curves, and E curves, with fragmented edges that look similar to a winding river, a grouping of clouds, or a forest. When we mimic the natural patterns found in nature, the curves and patterns we create are called configuration lines. When we look at nature, we notice that clusters of plants or trees are grouped together. For example, if we were to take a hike in the foothills of a mountain, we would notice grasses, shrubs, and wildflowers growing within their own groups. The groupings occur with deciduous trees and pines, each forming a cluster, whether large or small. Groups touch and intermingle at the edges. Some groups may be scattered about among other groups, such as wildflowers or shrubs, almost as if they were accents to the design.

When we think about designing our own gardens, we want them to reflect the Creator's method of design. This approach will bring out the natural beauty in the plants and give them an opportunity to shine as the Creator intended.

On Temple Square, flowers are arranged in patterns that look as if nature scattered seeds within the garden beds, and each plant just chose to grow where it landed. We call our design process "designing blind" because when we throw out the young bedding plants or bulbs to be planted, they are not in bloom and the color of

Nature designs in explosions, curves, and fragmented edges that look like a winding river, a grouping of clouds, or a forest.

Configurations that don't work

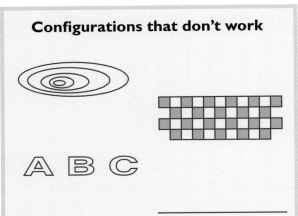

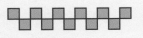

Nature has her own style and never places vegetation in straight lines, concentric circles, checkerboards, or zipper patterns.

Configurations that work

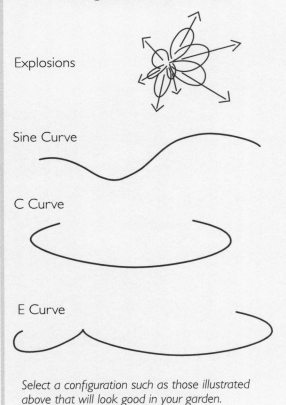

Explosions

Sine Curve

C Curve

E Curve

Select a configuration such as those illustrated above that will look good in your garden.

their flowers is not visible. To carry out a design, we must follow design principles rather than look at colors. We use four basic design principles at Temple Square to create our gardens. They are skeleton, tendon, flesh, and sparkle.

SKELETON

Dominance is the main design principle in the first step of the skeleton principle. In the garden, dominance in design is shown by plant form, texture, color, or position. Some characteristics that can qualify a plant as skeletal are the following:

- Strong, tall, vertical (for dominant form).
- Broad and dramatic (for dominant form).
- Coarse texture (for dominant texture).
- Vivid, bright blossoms or leaves (for dominant color).

If we choose plant form as the dominant feature in creating the skeleton, we would select plants like cleome (spider plant), digitalis (foxglove), or delphinium, which are dominant in their shape. If we choose texture as the skeleton in our garden design, we would pick plants such as hosta, ferns, or begonia, which are known for their interesting leaf textures. If we select color as the skeleton, we would think of color in terms of bright versus subdued, yellow versus violet, white versus blue, or red versus wine. Finally, if we select the position of the plant as the skeleton of the design, we would place the plant in the most dominant position of the garden.

We can even wrap up all of these principles into one plant that serves as the skeleton of the garden design. For example, a red hollyhock may be placed in the most dominant spot in the bed. With its tall height, large woolly leaves, and brilliant hue, the red hollyhock provides dominant form, texture, and color.

Decide what will be the dominant feature in

your garden. After choosing your design principles (form, texture, color, or position), select a configuration. This could be a sine curve, a C curve, or an E curve. Draw that line in the soil, placing the skeletal flowers on the ground in a triangular shape with three unequal sides along the curved line. One side of that triangle is then used to form the base of the next triangle of a different size. This pattern continues throughout the design until it forms the configuration you have chosen.

One way to get a natural curve in your garden bed is to take your garden hose, lay it on the ground in the bed, give it a wiggle to form a natural curve, and use that as your skeleton line. At Temple Square we place the skeleton plants, while still in their pots, along the configuration line so we can move them about and determine the right spot before we plant them. Skeletal plants constitute 10 to 20 percent of the flowers used in the design for a particular space.

TENDON

The flowers that form the tendons of the design should be positioned after the skeleton plants have been placed. These flowers are chosen to connect and blend the skeletal flowers, helping to hold together the form of the skeleton. The tendon flowers will complement the skeletal flowers in accordance with the design principle you choose—the form might be shorter or less dominant, the texture might be softer or smaller, the color might contrast or complement. Examples of blending plants are salvias and cleome, snapdragons and foxglove, lisianthus and roses. Plants that exhibit color contrast (subdued versus bright) include coreopsis 'Moonbeam' (pale yellow) and coreopsis 'Sundancer' (bright yellow).

Keep in mind that the tendon connects the skeletal flowers while maintaining the configuration line. We place the tendon flowers in the design

Sine curves mimic patterns found in nature.

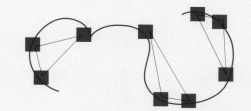

Skeletal flowers are placed on the ground in a triangular shape with three unequal sides along the curved line.

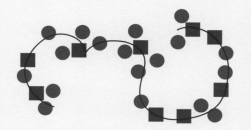

Tendon plants connect and blend with skeleton plants.

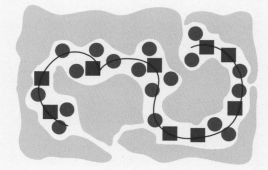

Flesh plants are all the remaining plants that fill in the bed.

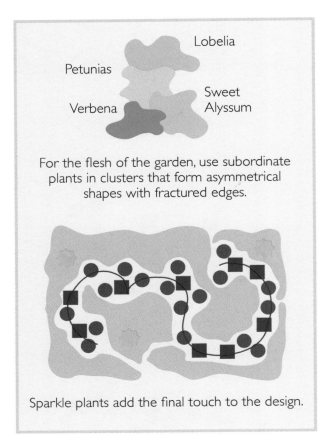

Petunias

Lobelia

Verbena

Sweet Alyssum

For the flesh of the garden, use subordinate plants in clusters that form asymmetrical shapes with fractured edges.

Sparkle plants add the final touch to the design.

colored groupings of pansies. Then set the groups of different colors side by side as you put them into the bed around the skeletal and tendon flowers. The flesh plants may constitute 60 to 80 percent of the total number of plants.

SPARKLE

Sparkle is the final touch we add to our design. It comes from a few special or highly contrasting orange, white, or yellow flowers. We set these plants out in odd-numbered groups of three, five, or seven, placing them randomly like lone wildflowers in a field of grass.

VARIETIES AND NUMBERS

A well-designed bed of flowers will always have a wide variety of plants within its design. On Temple Square, we try to use at least fifteen to thirty different varieties of plants in each flower bed. This helps preserve and hold together the garden design so that if a few flowers are crushed by a rolling ball or a running dog, the design will not be destroyed. Also, if a particular disease or insect attacks and you lose some plants, the wide variety of flowers will help ensure that most of your garden will survive. So if you want a bed that is saturated with the color red, find and plant a wide variety of plants with red blossoms. This will give the bed more texture and interest and reduce the risk that a disease or insect could wipe out a specific plant variety and destroy your design.

One way to determine the number of plants you need to fill a bed is to measure the bed's square footage and plan for 2 annuals per square foot or 1 perennial per 1 or 1½ square feet. For instance, if you have a 10-by-10-foot bed (100 square feet), you will need 200 annuals (100 x 2) or 100 to 150 perennials (100 x 1 or 100 x 1.5) to

so that their triangles interlock with the skeleton plant triangles along the configuration line. The tendon plants should constitute 10 to 20 percent of the total number of flowers in the design.

FLESH

The flesh plants are placed in the garden next. These are the more subordinate flowers such as alyssum, lobelia, and pansies. The flesh plants are scattered in and among the other flowers to complete and fill out the design. We place these plants in clusters that form asymmetrical shapes with fractured edges, and then we group them together to form clusters in and around the skeletal and tendon flowers to create a shifting mosaic with the groupings of plants.

For instance, you might make small, different-

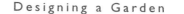

properly fill the bed. Of course, annuals and perennials can be mixed in equivalent ratios. Allow for about thirty different varieties of flowers within the bed. If you want a bed that has both bulbs and plants, plan for half the bed to be bulbs and the other half to be plants.

MARKER AND UNDERSTORY PLANTS

Marker plants are plants such as perennials that stay full within the garden throughout the growing season and are used to remind you where you have planted bulbs and other plants that die back to the ground before the season is over. Examples include the following:

- English daisy
- Hostas
- Heather
- Aubrieta
- Arabis
- Phlox
- Daphne
- Daylily

Evergreen shrubs, roses, and some ground covers also work well.

Understory plants are planted under a canopy of taller flowers and are usually the flesh of the garden. They give the bed a full and plentiful feeling. They also help crowd out weeds. Examples include the following:

- Aubrieta
- Pansy
- Viola
- Basket-of-gold
- Linaria
- Primrose
- Candytuft
- English daisy
- Forget-me-nots
- Phlox
- Hellebores
- Poppies
- Petunias

Set out sparkle plants in groups of three, five, or seven. In this flower bed, white fiberous begonia and yellow 'Moonbeam' coreopsis create highlights.

Geranium, 'Lemon Gem' marigold, 'White Star' zinnia, and 'Victoria Blue' salvia make great marker plants.

Understory plants, such as the purple arabis, white aubrieta, and basket-of-gold shown here, give the bed a full feeling while crowding out weeds.

IMPLEMENTING DESIGN PRINCIPLES IN A HOME GARDEN

After preparing your soil, begin the design process by determining the square footage of your garden space by multiplying garden width by garden length. If, for example, you have a garden area that measures 10 feet by 10 feet, your garden will be 100 square feet.

To simplify your design, let's say you decide to create a garden that will bloom during the summer season. If you were planting only annual flowers, you would need 200 plants (2 per square foot). If you decide that 20 percent of your garden area will be skeleton plants and another 20 percent will be tendon plants, you will need 40 skeleton plants (20 percent of 200) and 40 tendon plants (20 per-

cent of 200). That leaves 60 percent of your garden for flesh, which means your garden will have 120 flesh plants (60 percent of 200), of which about 15 will be used for sparkle.

If you're going to use perennials in your garden design, remember that you need fewer per square foot (1 to 1.5) than you do annuals (2). Let's say you decide to use perennials as your garden's skeleton and tendon and that you simplify things by deciding to use 1 perennial per square foot.

To fill the same 100-square-foot garden, you again decide that 20 percent of your garden (20 square feet) will be skeleton and 20 percent will be tendon. This time, however, you need only 20 perennials for skeleton and 20 perennials for tendon (1 plant per square foot rather than 2). That leaves 60 percent of the garden for flesh. If you decide to fill the remaining space with annuals (2 per square foot), you will again need 120 flesh plants (2 x 60), a few of which will be sparkle.

At this point in your design, choose a color scheme (see section below) and determine what types of plants (sun or shade) you need in your garden. Remember to use a wide variety of plants in your design, including both annuals and perennials. Also, choose plants that bloom at different times throughout the summer. Select a wide variety of perennials with staggered bloom times to give your garden color all season.

As you place each of the layers of design in your garden, walk around the bed and examine your design from different angles, looking for balance and interest. A good garden design does not need to have all the tall flowers in the middle and all the short flowers on the edges. Nature mixes up plant heights and textures. So have fun, and get a little dirty!

As you watch your garden grow and develop, take pictures and keep a garden journal. Then, during the winter, review what transpired and determine what changes to make next spring and summer. Visit other gardens in your area, looking for successful ideas worth emulating. Also, be sure to read garden magazines and books (see our favorite list in chapter 9). A gardener always benefits by gaining more knowledge.

COLOR THEORY

From the time we open our eyes in the morning until we go to sleep at night, we are surrounded by color. We may not realize it, but color affects our emotions.

The colors with which we surround ourselves say much about our personality. When choosing a color scheme to use in your garden, start with the mood you would like to create and then look at

A good garden design does not need to have all the tall flowers in the middle and all the short flowers on the edges. Nature mixes up plant heights and textures, similar to the effect achieved by interspersing tulips, pansies, and lamium.

Various shades of pink nicotiana, vinca, chrysanthemum, and roses combine harmoniously with 'Victoria Blue' salvia and 'Johnson's Blue' geranium.

your favorite colors. Some designers use colored tissue paper in designing a garden so they can see the colors as they put them together. If the colors you choose work together to create the mood you want, you are ready to choose plants. If not, decide whether mood or color is most important, and work around that choice. Don't be afraid to experiment because trial and error is often the best teacher.

The effects of color in a garden are somewhat different than in other settings. Remember that outdoor colors in the early morning seem different than in the hot afternoon. In the less-intense light of the morning and evening, colors appear much softer than during the intense light of midday.

Nothing in a garden will have more impact than color. Remember the phrase, "We see red when we are angry." Red has been shown to raise blood pressure and heart rate. "We seem blue when we are sad" is another phrase that refers to color moods. Actually, blue can provide a calm, serene feeling. Green is considered the most restful color. Yellow reminds people of happiness and energy, while orange stimulates and energizes.

The Color Wheel

To implement a design most effectively, it is important to understand the universal color wheel and how colors relate to one another.

A color wheel can help you effectively implement a design.

Definitions

Primary colors: red, yellow, and blue; they cannot be mixed from other colors.

Secondary colors: two primary colors mixed together resulting in orange, green, or violet.

Tertiary (intermediate) colors: one primary color and one secondary color next to each other on the color wheel that are mixed together (example: green + yellow = yellow-green).

Advancing (warm) colors: reds, oranges, and yellows.

Receding (cool) colors: greens, blues, and violets.

Hue: another name for color.

Tint: color + white.

Tone: color + gray.

Shade: color + black.

Chroma or intensity: the brightness or dullness of a color.

Value: the lightness or darkness of a color.

Complementary colors: combining a shade, tint, or tone of one color with the opposite color on the color wheel; complementary colors signify agreement and resolution (example: blue and orange).

Contrasting colors: one-third of the color wheel over in either direction from one color will yield a contrasting color; contrasting colors signify high energy, action, and vigor (example: yellow and red).

Monochromatic: any shade, tint, or tone of one color.

Achromatic: a colorless scheme using blacks, whites, and grays.

Analogous: using two or more shades, tints, or tones that are next to each other on the color wheel; analogous colors create a feeling that is peaceful and restful (example: green and blue).

Warm colors require skill to artfully combine and use.

Cool colors create a soothing, restful mood.

Color and light: subdued evening lighting and candlelight create a distortion of color; under these circumstances, light colors need more intensity while dark colors need less.

Color and distance: distance causes receding (cool) colors to black out; consequently, lighter values of color should be employed for greater emphasis.

Color and ratio: color has visual weight; darker colors appear to be heavier than lighter colors.

Key color: the dominant color in a color scheme.

Character: the mood or message conveyed by color.

Warm and Cool Colors

Color can suggest feelings of warmth or coolness, which can affect our mood. The six main sectors of the color wheel are divided into orange, red, yellow, green, blue, and violet. Orange, red, and yellow are warm colors. Their brightness and intensity seem to jump out at you from flower beds, giving the impression that the flowers are closer than they really are. This can make a garden seem smaller than it actually is. You may prefer using a smaller amount of warm colors than other more subdued colors.

The difference between too much and too little color can be likened to personality. An outgoing, exciting individual can be fun to be around. An obnoxious, loud individual quickly wears out his welcome.

Warm colors are powerful colors that take some skill to artfully combine and use. Orange and yellow columbine, red snapdragons, red hot pokers, dahlias, yellow yarrows, fennel, mulleins, and orange wallflowers are examples of warm-colored flowers. The trick to using warm colors is to combine them with a high proportion of green leaves and paler yellows and oranges. Brilliant and intense colors create emphasis, while their lighter relatives serve to blend and unify design.

Cool colors are green, blue, and violet. They create a soothing, restful mood. These colors tend to recede into the distance, helping a small garden appear larger. In shady areas, they tend to disappear into the shadows, so they are seen and appreciated better in sunny locations. Cool colors blend

This grass garden located south of the Salt Lake Temple shows the importance of form and texture in a monochromatic color scheme.

A pastel mix of pink ageratum, silver artemisia, lavender lobelia, 'Victoria Blue' salvia, and deep purple heliatrope can be seen in the Kimball Cemetery, located east of the Church Office Building.

and unify a garden. When using flowers with bright, intense colors, make sure you use a cool color directly behind them to soften and unify.

Primary and Secondary Colors

Red. Red, usually considered a hot color, adds brightness to the waning days of summer. But red also comes in many soothing shades, such as pink, burgundy, and maroon. Because red provides emphasis, focus, and accent, it should not be over-used in a small garden. Examples of red flowers include tulips, roses, peonies, and geraniums.

Yellow. Most people like yellow but find it too strong for their taste unless it is a pastel hue, such as a lemon yellow. So many yellow flowers are available that you can easily overdo this color in your garden. A few examples of yellow flowers are coreopsis, gaillardia, black-eyed Susan, marigold, and snapdragon.

Blue. It's hard to come by a true blue in the garden, but many plants bloom in various shades of blue. Blue works well with most colors. When combined with orange, which is the opposite of blue on the color wheel, blue creates excitement. Blue and red flowers, such as red dianthus with blue lobelia, augment and enhance each other. (For a regal touch, add some purple nearby.) Blue and yellow flowers like lavender and coreopsis are popular together and can be seen in several gardens on the three blocks of Temple Square. Blue can also be used to help blend colors that clash.

Orange. Orange is a hard color to use, but a little bit can really enhance or add sparkle to a garden. Orange looks good with blue, purple, and shades of yellow and bronzy brown. Good examples are the orange and yellow zinnia, gaillardia, calendula, and tulip.

Green. The presence of green is central to a garden's color scheme. An expanse of fresh green grass sets off a flower bed and gives the eye a

The lime-green hues of coleus, which is grown for its beautiful foliage, contrasts well with the deeper green shades in the leaves of the impatiens.

restful break from a profusion of border colors. Several plants are grown for their beautiful foliage rather than for the color of their blooms. Bells of Ireland, hostas, ferns, and variegated foliage are a few examples to consider for your garden.

Violet (purple). Violet signifies luxury or royalty, especially in its darker values. Violet is a rich color known as the queen of color. Violets and purples were hard to find in the distant past, which made them a favorite of royalty. Violet hues give the garden designer several options. From lavender to plum, violet can be used as either a bold accent or a soft accent. Often it is important to balance the heaviness of violet with other colors. Gray and silver foliage enliven deep violet hues that tend to recede in shaded areas.

White. Pure white is at its best in a shaded garden, where the brightness is welcome. It is most effective when used with variegated green foliage. As Louise Beebe Wilder said in her book *Color in My Garden,* "White used in broad masses has dignity and a serene beauty, but spotted all about the garden is simply a stirrer up of factions, setting the flowers against one another instead of drawing them into happy relationships" (New York City: Atlantic Monthly Press, 1990, 8).

Basic Color Schemes

A short discussion of three basic color schemes—monochromatic, analogous, and complementary—will help illustrate how color theory works in designing a flower bed.

Monochromatic. Monochromatic color schemes take one color and play with its various tints and shades. Using a single color is a subtle technique that creates a restful feeling in the garden and focuses attention on form and texture.

Examples of complementary colors are red and green. The red-leafed coleus contrasts and complements the green foliage of campanula, begonia, and ageratum.

Using lighter tints of complementary colors is an effective way to soften a garden that might be too vibrant. Pale yellow narcissus and lavender pansies create less impact than bright yellow mixed with deep purple.

The shapes of flowers and plants become more noticeable when colors are more subdued. It takes sensibility and understanding of texture and form to create a successful monochromatic garden that avoids monotony.

Analogous. Analogous color schemes combine neighboring colors on the color wheel in a harmonious fashion. Flowers in blues, blue violets, violets, and pink create a blend of related hues that are analogous. Varying the value of these colors, using lighter tints and darker shades, adds interest to the garden.

A good way for beginners to start designing their garden is to begin with pastels and experiment with occasional accents of stronger, darker colors. One caution about designing with pastel colors, however, is that they often look bland. Analogous color schemes have been important on Temple Square, particularly when used to create a

contrast against the gray granite buildings. A good example of using pastel colors with stronger colors can be found during the summer in the south center mall at Temple Square.

Complementary. Complementary color schemes join opposites on the color wheel—orange and blue, yellow and violet, red and green—for maximum contrast. When colors are of equal value, the results are electric. Some might say that using strong complementary colors can result in a garden that is too vibrant. Using a lighter tint of one color and a medium shade of the contrasting color can reduce the extreme effect of contrasting color combinations. As you experiment with different color schemes, you will find some that are more successful than others. It is largely a matter of personal taste. Have fun with different combinations to see what happens. Be sure to record your successes and failures for next year's garden. ❧

Chapter 5

Bulbs, Spring Flowers, Shrubs, and Trees

Each spring the Temple Square gardens come alive with an incredible array of tulips, daffodils, hyacinths, and other bulbs that burst into bloom well before most perennials. Spring-flowering bulbs signal the beginning of the growing season as they fill the bare winter ground with resplendent color. Temple Square gardens also feature summer- and fall-blooming bulbs, but they are fewer in variety and must compete with perennial and annual flowers for attention.

Temple Square is the state's top tourist attraction, with visitors coming throughout the year. But because many Latter-day Saints assemble in Salt Lake City for general conference the first weekend in April, they would be unable to enjoy the true potential of Temple Square if its gardens depended on summer annual flowers only.

Over the years the Temple Square gardening staff has "invented" spring-blooming gardens for Utah. This invention came after years of study, trial, and error, and searching for the right way to grow plants in spring gardens. In this chapter, we share what they have learned. Many gardeners persist in waiting until spring before planting their spring gardens. But years of experience have taught us that procrastination does not work. Almost all spring bulbs must go through the rigors of winter before they can bloom. The same goes for other spring flowers.

Waiting until the soil dries out in the spring before planting pansies and other spring flowers means that by the time they finally become established, it's almost time to take them out. Fall planting lets them establish a good root system so that they're ready to burst into color when winter snows finally disappear.

The gardens at Temple Square are noted more for their spring displays than for their summer flowers. However, large gardens with spectacular plantings of tulips and other spring bulbs face a special dilemma in Utah: unpredictable and changeable spring weather. As a result, flowers don't always bloom on cue at a certain date.

Since it is nearly impossible to time the bloom of bulbs to April conference, spring flower gardens in Utah require variety in order to be successful. That means adding trees, shrubs, and other spring flowers to the mix.

Tulips provide a welcome burst of spring color on Temple Square.

Although bulbs are truly spectacular flowers, they cannot sustain a garden for the entire gardening season. In fact, most spring bulbs look great for a week, good for two weeks, and fair for three weeks. They then become nothing more than dead petals, gangling flower stems, and long leaves that eventually turn brown and die.

The salvation of a spring garden is found in the other plants we grow. These include winter annuals, biennials that take two years to complete their life cycle, and spring-blooming perennials that come back again and again. All share a common characteristic of being able to survive the winter and thrive in early spring.

PLANTING YOUR SPRING GARDEN

Preparing Temple Square gardens in October for the spring bulb and flower displays often raises concern among some visitors. "Why are you taking out those perfectly good flowers before they have been killed by the frost?" they ask the gardeners. Long experience has taught us that there truly is "a time to plant, and a time to pluck up that which is planted" (Ecclesiastes 3:2).

Like spring weather, fall weather is unpredictable. But we needn't wait for the first killing frost before planting our spring garden. Nothing is quite as discouraging as trying to clear away the snow so we can plant spring bulbs and other flowers. Knowing how, what, and when to plant will make the difference between a few days of spring color and blooms that last.

At Temple Square, we replace our gardens each October after general conference. Anticipate your fall tear-out and planting date when the luster starts to fade from your summer annuals. Planting spring bloomers so they can establish a good root system before winter arrives prevents plants from being pushed out of the ground by repeated freezing and thawing—a process known as frost heaving. Plants that are heaved out by frost dry out and die.

Fall-planted flowers fall into different botanical categories. Despite their botanical definitions, we sometimes use these plants differently than nature intended. For example, pansies are biennials, but we grow them as winter annuals. We're not interested in having them produce seed, and they do not withstand the heat of summer. Flower breeders have also changed the way some of these flowers perform when compared to native-grown varieties.

BULBS

The term *bulb* refers to a broad category of plants with fleshy underground stems and roots. They are dormant for much of the year but send up leaves and flowers during their blooming period. This category of plants includes the following:

- Bulbs—fleshy, underground scales with any embryonic plant inside. Tulips and alliums are true bulbs.
- Corms—modified stem tissue that is flattened on top. Corms shrivel during the growing season and produce new corms around the original corm. Gladiolus and crocuses are examples of corms.
- Rhizomes—underground stems with multiple tips. Bearded iris and cannas grow from rhizomes.
- Tubers—swollen stems that are covered with buds, or eyes. Tuberous begonias and potatoes grow from tubers.
- Tuberous roots—swollen roots that resemble tubers but are more rounded. Dahlias and sweet potatoes grow from tuberous roots.

Spring bulbs are truly the harbingers of spring.

Snowdrops and crocuses often poke their heads out from underneath the snow. An assortment of flowers of all sizes, shapes, colors, and descriptions follows them. With proper planning, it's possible to have spring bulbs in bloom for several months.

The beautiful spring bulbs on Temple Square include tulips, daffodils, hyacinths, and numerous other bulbs with spectacular blooms. The unfortunate downside of these bulbs is that their blossoms do not last. After blooming, their foilage is rather nondescript and unattractive, especially when it is dying back.

Creative gardeners solve the problem in two ways. First, they orchestrate the blooming of bulbs so the flowering lasts from snowmelt to late spring. For example, they select early tulips, mid-season tulips, and late-season tulips. Second, they use an abundance of understory plants. They also plant bulbs that will change their garden's color emphasis. For example, their flower beds start with predominant orange and purple crocuses but are followed by yellow and white daffodils.

Bulbs must be left in the ground until the foliage dies down, so our gardeners hide the dying foliage with other desirable plants. These winter annuals, biennials, and perennials are selected for their spring bloom period and winter hardiness. Because most bulbs are accustomed to spending the summer in a warm, dry, dormant condition, they survive well if you dig them up after they bloom. You can then replant them in the fall after you take out your summer garden.

Caring for Bulbs

We want our flowers to look their best for the millions of people who visit Temple Square each year, so we do things differently from most home gardeners. First, we remove almost all our bulbs. Leaving them in over the summer encourages

Planting bulbs that grow to different heights creates depth and adds interest to your garden design.

decay and interferes with other garden work. Because color and design play such a major part in our gardens, we plant new bulbs each year in our most visible flower beds. Labor costs are too high to justify sorting and saving bulbs. However, many bulbs are replanted in less visible gardens.

We don't leave bulbs in the ground as long as you might at home. Ideally, bulbs should be left in home flower beds until their foliage starts to turn yellow. They can then be cut back or dug out and stored. Leaving the foliage in place allows bulbs to store a maximum amount of energy, encouraging return bloom the following year.

Bulbs are not as showy during subsequent blooms, but for home gardens they're worth digging up, sorting, and saving. After discarding the ones that are shriveled, moldy, or otherwise damaged, allow them to dry out before storing them in a cool, dry place until fall. Then replant them. If you see evidence of insects, treat the bulbs with bulb dust. Discard bulbs that show signs of disease.

Good Signs	Bad Signs
Stem growth is absent, although a short, thick shoot tip is acceptable.	Existing stem growth is long, spindly, and white or pale green.
Neck is firm.	Neck is soft and diseased.
Surface is clean and firm.	Surface is dirty and soft.
Bulb is heavy for its size.	Bulb is light for its size.
Tunic is intact, although cracks or gaps in tulip skin are acceptable.	Tunic is missing, or tissue underneath is diseased, moldy, damaged, or shriveled.
Root growth is not apparent.	Root growth is clearly active.
Base is firm (test with finger) and free of rot.	Base is soft and shows signs of rot.

To keep your spring garden showy, add new bulbs to your fall plantings each year. Adding new bulbs is how we create the magnificent spring gardens at Temple Square.

Buying Bulbs

The best way to ensure that you'll get good blooms is to select high-quality bulbs. Generally, bulb size is directly proportional to bloom size. Small bulbs, which often do not bloom the first year, are usually a disappointment.

Choose firm bulbs that are free of deep cuts or scars, and avoid bulbs that are badly molded or discolored. A bulb's paper-like covering, the tunic, is not essential for growth, so don't be concerned if it's torn or missing.

Watch out for inexpensive bulbs and advertisements promoting hundreds of bulbs at a low price. These "great deals" include a few tulips, daffodils, and other desirable bulbs; however, grape hyacinth, Star-of-Bethlehem, and other bulbs that spread and become weedy usually comprise the bulk.

Always examine loose bulbs closely before you buy. Remember that a poor-quality bulb will never produce a good-quality bloom.

Planting Bulbs

Poor planting techniques have a direct effect on bulb growth and survival. Plant bulbs at a depth approximately three times their diameter. Shallow planting causes frost heaving. Deeper planting prevents heaving and protects bulbs from surface digging if you plant annuals over them during the summer.

Bulbs tolerate a wide variety of soils and locations except for heavy clay with poor drainage. Gardeners afflicted with heavy clay soils should plant bulbs in raised beds or berms. For planting in clay

Hyacinth bulbs are carefully laid out before any other bulbs are thrown. Be sure to wear gloves when touching hyacinths, which can cause skin irritation.

In the fall, Temple Square gardeners throw out spring-flowering bulbs first and then fill in the empty spaces with pansies or other spring bloomers. Laying out the plants before they are dug into the ground helps designers visualize their intended design.

An array of perky pansies is ready to be transplanted in the garden. The big, deep flats can better accommodate developing root systems.

Bulbs are placed in a generous sine line before other spring plants are added to the design.

A meandering path of yellow narcissus takes center stage in this spring garden, dotted with aurinia, pansies, and aubrieta.

soils, mix in large amounts of coarse organic matter to improve drainage and aeration.

Plant tulip bulbs as soon as the soil starts to cool in the fall. This will give the tiny embryo plants inside the bulbs the chance to develop a good root system before the soil freezes. A good root system ensures larger, more attractive flowers in the spring. Bulb blooms look better if planted in clusters or groups rather than in single file.

You can find bulbs adapted to rock gardens, foundation plantings, shrubbery areas, flower beds, and rose gardens. Bulbs do best in areas of full sun or moderate shade. They will not rebloom in deep shade.

Bulb Problems

When grown in normal, well-drained soil, bulbs have few problems with disease. Bulb diseases are usually serious only if you overwater.

Some gardeners complain that the tulips they

Use a wide variety of spring-flowering bulbs and plants for a profusion of color and texture. Tulips mix well with white arabis, purple aubrieta, basket-of-gold, and pink bleeding hearts.

painstakingly plant in the fall don't come up in the spring with their daffodils. If you're experiencing this problem, you can likely blame mice, squirrels, or deer. Animals leave daffodils and hyacinths alone because they're poisonous, but they find tulips tasty. Unfortunately, there are no safe, effective methods for keeping these animals out of your tulips. Fence your garden or cover the beds with netting or chicken wire to discourage these pests.

Fertilizing Bulbs

Spring-flowering bulbs need no fertilizer for their first season of blooming. They already contain all the food and energy they need for a healthy season of growth. Fertilizing stimulates growth for return bloom, so fertilizing after flowering is more helpful than fertilizing at planting. Add manure or commercial bulb fertilizer in the spring of the second year when the first shoots appear. Compost and other amendments also benefit bulbs.

For many years phosphorus or bonemeal was highly promoted as bulb food, but recent research

has shown that bulbs use as much if not more nitrogen than phosphorus. The best solution is a fertile soil.

OTHER SPRING FLOWERS

The secret to creating a beautiful, long-lasting spring garden that looks good through all kinds of weather is selecting the right plants. It's essential that you use plants that grow well in the winter, including winter annuals, biennials, spring-blooming perennials, woody plants, and flowering trees and shrubs.

These plants provide a wonderful backdrop for your bulbs as their blooms come and go. For example, spring perennials provide a nice transition from spring blooms to summer flowers, covering bulb foliage in the process. Many spring perennials also offer attractive ground cover after they bloom. Some aggressive plants need grooming to make room for summer annuals, but others die back.

Fall-planted selections that bloom in the Temple Square gardens in the spring include the following:

Pansies. Pansies are stellar performers in spring gardens. In the fall, we transplant them into the gardens of Temple Square, where they continue to grow during the winter, even under the snow. As spring approaches, pansies are covered with abundant blooms that show until they're removed to make room for summer annuals. Pansies don't tolerate summer heat, but few spring flowers rival these biennials in color or length of bloom season.

We recommend large-sized pansy plants in big, deep flats that better accommodate their developing root systems. These plants adapt better once the weather turns cold. Smaller plants with smaller root systems often end up heaving out of the ground.

Pansies are stronger than their name implies. Planted in the fall, they continue to grow throughout the winter, even under snow.

A generous mulch layer around plants insulates them, keeping them from drying out and preventing them from heaving. If the weather remains warm and dry after you've planted your pansies, water them. Remember that snow does not hurt these hardy plants. Rather, it serves as an insulating blanket, preventing them from drying out.

They come in a wide range of colors, including red, purple, blue, bronze, pink, black, yellow, white, and lavender.

Violas. Violas are often considered miniature pansies. Johnny-jump-up violas are the best choice for spring blooms. They complement bulbs in rock gardens, and they often reseed themselves and naturalize where they're planted.

Wallflowers (*Erysimum,* syn. *Cheiranthus*). Wallflowers come in red, white, yellow, cream, pink, and purple. They are one of the most underused of all spring-blooming flowers, but they are worth planting because of the beauty they add to spring gardens.

Iceland poppies (*Papaver nudicaule*). Iceland poppies are another wonderful spring performer. Their large, delicate flowers do best during cool, sunny springs. They display shades of red, pink, white, orange, and yellow. They are perennials, so they can be left in year after year. We use them at Temple Square as winter annuals, which means they are planted in the fall and bloom in the spring.

Dianthus. These flowers come in many varieties. They too are used as winter annuals on Temple Square and create beautiful, long-lasting spring displays. Brilliant displays of white, pink, red, lavender, maroon, and mixtures of these colors appear soon after the snow melts.

Forget-me-nots (*Myosotis sylvatica*). Forget-me-nots produce clusters of tiny blue, pink, or white flowers in the early spring.

Brunnera (*Siberian bugloss*). Brunnera is a spring-blooming perennial with flowers similar to

Bleeding hearts are one of the earliest perennials to bloom in the spring. Their arching sprays are strung with dancing, white-tipped blossoms, laced with fernlike leaves.

The patio area behind the Lion House provides a protected environment for this spring-flowering dogwood.

forget-me-nots. Choose it for areas that are not going to be replanted each year.

Lunaria. Lunaria, also known as honesty or money plant, has beautiful lavender, purple, or white flowers. It is slightly taller than other flowers and is best used as background or with other tall flowers. After the blossoms fade, they take on the appearance of translucent silver circles, from which they get their "money" moniker.

Foxglove. This biennial grows three to four feet high after spending its first year as a small rosette. The second season it sends up spectacular flower stocks covered with funnel-shaped blooms that open first at the bottom of the spike and continue blooming up the entire length of the stem.

Lupines. Lupines produce a showy spike of flowers similar to foxglove. They range in color from white to pink, lavender, and other pastels.

Stocks. Stocks bloom well in early spring. They were once grown extensively for use in cut-flower arrangements but have enjoyed a resurgence in spring gardens.

Other perennials that give a beautiful spring

show include arabis, aubrieta, bleeding hearts, basket-of-gold, ajuga, primulas, and snapdragons.

FLOWERING SHRUBS AND TREES

Spring rebirth is made even more beautiful by magnificent flowering shrubs, or woody plants, that create splashes of color that contrast with the bright green of a resurrecting garden. Attractive spring gardens depend on flowering trees and shrubs to add variety and vertical appeal. Shrubs add form and attractive blooms, while small trees add form, blooms, and foliage.

As you select woody plants and trees, look for those that offer more than just spring color. Strength, health, and form are equally important. Blooms are secondary if a shrub or tree does not grow well or look attractive in your landscape.

Shrubs

Forsythia. The earliest shrubs to show their blossoms in our gardens are the forsythias. These plants brave the spring frosts but often lose their flowers because they bloom so early. When not flowering, forsythias are plain shrubs with medium-green leaves. They require severe pruning, tolerate most soils, like full sun, and grow best with moderate irrigation and fertilization. We use three species and many varieties on Temple Square, including dwarf forms for small beds.

Spirea. Spireas are hardy shrubs that vary in form, height, and flowering season, but all provide generous quantities of pink, white, lavender, or reddish flowers. Temple Square gardens feature spring-flowering varieties, but summer- and fall-blooming varieties are also available.

Mock orange. Mock orange is a white-flowering spring shrub. It blooms late in the spring and is covered with fragrant blossoms that smell like orange blossoms. These shrubs prefer full sun and tolerate most normal growing conditions. They come in several species and varieties.

Our gardens feature several other spring-flowering shrubs, including lilacs and several species of honeysuckle that produce beautiful, fragrant flowers. They also feature trees that burst into wave after wave of beautiful showy blossoms.

Trees

Crabapple. Crabapple is one of the small, versatile trees we use in our gardens. Crabapples are cold hardy and grow well. They come in many shapes, ranging from narrow upright forms to pendulous weeping forms. Crabapple flowers are single or double, large or small, and come in white, pink, red, lavender, or a combination of these colors. Tree foliage ranges from bright to glossy green to shades of red, bronze, and purple. Crabapple trees are susceptible to disease and can produce messy fruit, so choose varieties carefully.

Cherry. Flowering cherry trees come in dozens of different varieties, including spreading trees, trees with weeping forms, and trees with narrow, upright columnar shapes. Their flowers are single or double and come in white, pink, or magenta. Hardy varieties include 'Schubert's' or 'Canada Red' chokecherry, which produce red to purplish foliage in the summer.

Flowering plum. Flowering plums are showy but have several problems, so we do not use them extensively on Temple Square. Some are not reliably hardy, even in warmer areas. In addition, they have thick, upright growth with narrow branch angles that break easily with snow or heavy winds.

Hawthorn. Hawthorns come in numerous sizes, shapes, and colors. Choose improved varieties that are less susceptible to insects and disease. They require regular pruning to keep them looking good. One of our favorites is the Lavelle

hawthorn, which grows along South Temple Street in the planters in front of the Beehive and Lion Houses.

Horse chestnut. This tree is another favorite. It can produce showy white or red flowers, depending on the variety. It is widely cultivated as an ornamental shade tree.

Dogwood. Dogwood trees are uncommon to Utah, but we have a couple of them located in protected areas behind the Lion House. They have large, single, showy flowers. Dogwood will not tolerate heavy clay or alkaline soils.

Magnolia. Magnolias are also less common but grow in several protected locations on Temple Square. They require rich soil that is well drained and amended to reduce its pH. Flower colors are white, pink, red, and lavender. Magnolias have some of the largest and showiest blossoms of any of the spring-flowering trees.

A weeping cherry tree is adorned with cascading branches of pink flowers that bloom in early spring.

Chapter 6

Roses

Roses are the most popular flowering shrubs in Utah because they have a long bloom season, feature blossoms of varied color and size, and are easy to grow. The gardens at Temple Square feature an eclectic mix of rose bushes, but we give special consideration to roses that are durable and easy to grow.

Roses don't dominate any of the Temple Square flower gardens, but you'll see a variety of these delightful shrubs on the Conference Center roof gardens, between the Joseph Smith Memorial Building and the Church Administration Building, between the Tabernacle and the Assembly Hall, and in the Beehive House gardens. Taller varieties are used among tall plants and near walls. Smaller varieties and miniatures fit into border or container gardens and among lower plants. Roses add interest, fragrance, and variety to beds filled with summer flowers.

The timing of roses is just right. They steal the show in June while the annual beds are still working up to their full summer glory. After June, roses become a little more retiring and less showy, but they continue to produce flowers that spark up the beds throughout the summer. Our crews encourage continued blooming by clipping spent blooms to the first five-leaflet leaf below the blossom. A few weeks later, the bush produces a new rose to replace the removed blossom.

Rosebush names are as intriguing and diverse as roses themselves. Names like 'Cherish,' 'Carefree Beauty,' 'Little Sizzler,' 'Green Ice,' 'Angel Face,' 'Hot Tamale,' 'Heritage,' and 'Suzy Q' represent all

'Sweet Juliet' is a favorite English shrub rose with a vigorous growth habit. It is one of the few apricot-colored roses in the world.

types of roses—grandiflora, floribunda, shrubs, tea roses, and climbers. The selection of roses in the Temple Square gardens focus on color, variety, type, size, shape, and adaptability. Among the offerings, you'll find old roses with once-a-year blooms, fragrant roses, low-growing shrub varieties, and taller varieties.

BUYING

Rose plants are sold in three grades: No. 1, No. 1½, and No. 2. Grades are based on the size and number of canes. No. 1 roses are best and have at least three canes three-eighths of an inch or more in diameter. Top-grade plants produce superior blossoms, both in quality and quantity, and they produce them sooner than inferior

'Charlotte Armstrong' is a hybrid tea rose named for a family that pioneered the growing of roses in America.

The Nauvoo Rose, located by the east gate of the Beehive House, is said to have come to Utah as a transplant from Nauvoo, Illinois.

plants. Roses are sold bare root or as packaged plants with shavings around the base. Potted roses are often started in a greenhouse so that they are in bloom for early sales.

When purchasing a bare-root rose bush from a local nursery, make sure that the stems are green and not shriveled. Stems should not feel soft when squeezed between your fingers. The bush should have three or more stems that are at least a half-inch or larger in diameter. The stems should have no new growth, and the buds should be dormant. Early spring is a good time to purchase roses. The selection is at its best, and the plants have not gone through a long, hot summer in a container.

Most roses available in nurseries are grafted roses, which means a small piece of the desired variety has been grafted onto a wild vigorous rose. On Temple Square, however, we prefer to buy roses that are grown on their own root. Own-root roses have many advantages over grafted roses. They are more disease free, virus resistant, and winter hardy. If the own-root plant freezes, it can grow back the following spring true to the variety, while grafted roses usually die or send up suckers that may not be true to the desired variety. Own-root roses start out small and are a little more expensive than grafted roses, but they grow rapidly after they have become established. Own-root roses can live to one hundred years or more, while grafted roses may lose their vigor after ten to fifteen years. Sources for own-root roses can be found in chapter 10.

The cold hardiness of roses and rose rootstock varies considerably. Check local sources to make sure your selections are winter hardy. In areas with very cold winters, cover roses or mulch well to protect them.

Hybrid teas. Hybrid teas, the most widely grown roses, are available only as a grafted rose. They have showy blooms throughout the growing season. Plants grow from two to five feet high. Flowers may be single or double. Buds are long and pointed, with single flowers or clusters of three to five flowers per stem, which are used as ornamentals or cut flowers. Hybrid teas need protection in severe winters.

Floribunda. Floribunda rose flowers are similar in size, shape, and color to hybrid tea blossoms, with flowers appearing in clusters with short stems. Floribunda rose bushes are hardy, disease-resistant, low-growing shrubs. Use them in beds where you desire many flowers. Temple Square gardens feature several types of floribunda roses.

Grandiflora. Grandiflora roses are an offspring of hybrid tea roses. These flowers are borne singly or in clusters on longer stems. They resemble hybrid teas but are larger and grow three to six feet tall.

Miniature. Miniature roses are tiny versions of other roses. They grow less than two feet high and are often used in mass plantings or borders.

Shrub. Shrub roses are hardy, spreading plants that require little maintenance. Varieties grow four to twelve feet tall with many canes and thick foliage. Flowers can be single or double and are borne at the ends of the canes or on branches along the canes. Some flower once in the spring while others flower continuously. These easy-care plants are grown extensively on the Conference Center roof because they bloom for most of the summer and tolerate heat, drought, and wind.

Heritage. Heritage, or "old" roses, are those grown before 1867. Albas, Bourbons, Damasks, Mosses, Noisettes, and Rugosas are heritage roses, as are wild and shrub roses such as the 'Nootka Rose' (Rosa woodsii), 'Austrian Copper' (Rosa foetida bicolor), 'Father Hugo' (Rosa hugonis), and many others. For the most part, these are hardy, drought-tolerant, pest-resistant plants that bloom only in the spring.

Climbing and rambler. Climbing and rambler roses have long, arching canes. The bushes don't actually climb and must be attached to trellises, arbors, or fences. Climbing roses have many different colors and types of blooms. Large flowered climbers have thick, stiff canes up to ten feet long, with flowers that bloom through the summer and fall. Ramblers have long, thin canes and

'Green Ice' is an excellent miniature rose with glossy leaves and pale green blooms that fade to white.

A hardy floribunda rose, 'Gruss an Aachen' produces abundant blooms throughout the summer.

small clusters of flowers that bloom in early summer.

Tree. Tree roses are classified by growth form rather than by flower type. They are created by grafting bush roses onto an upright trunk. Use them as accents in formal gardens or as specimen plants. Tree roses are not cold hardy and need special winter protection.

Planting Roses

When planting roses, prune to the three or four healthiest canes, and cut canes to twelve inches long and one-quarter inch above an outward-facing bud.

Dig holes large enough to accommodate roots without crowding, and make a small mound of soil to support the roots.

Add soil and then add water to firm the soil and eliminate air pockets.

PLANTING

Roses tolerate many soils and climates but do best in light, well-drained soils. Use raised planters or beds when planting roses in poorly drained or salty soils. Problem soils cause root rot and micronutrient deficiencies. Avoid areas with difficult-to-control perennial weeds such as field bindweed, white top, or quack grass. Roses need at least six hours of full sun a day. Air movement discourages diseases, but heavy winds can damage blossoms. Roses grow best by themselves because other plants compete for light, water, and nutrients.

Successful growing starts with correct planting techniques. Dig a hole large enough to accommodate roots without crowding. Soak bare root roses for twelve to twenty-four hours before planting. Inside the hole, plant bare-root roses on a soil cone that supports the bud at the correct height. In Utah, set the bud two inches below the soil level to prevent winter kill. One disadvantage of burying bud unions is that suckers and crown gall (a bacterial disease) become more difficult to control.

Prune the plant to the three or four healthiest canes spaced around the plant. (Purchased plants have already been pruned.) Cut canes to twelve inches long and one-quarter inch above an outward facing bud. Remove broken, dead, or diseased roots, and set the plant in place. Add soil and water to firm the soil and eliminate air pockets. Plant potted roses the same way after inspecting them for girdling or encircling roots. If plants are root bound, cut one-inch deep slits down the side of the root ball to eliminate potential problems.

Water every seven to ten days. Overwatering is a major cause of death of newly planted roses. Roses tolerate drought, but lack of water impairs flower quality and quantity. Roses benefit from a thick mulch layer to hold moisture and prevent weeds. Use wood chips, bark, compost, sawdust, or similar products.

PRUNING

Pruning improves plant appearance and health by removing dead, diseased, weak, and broken wood. It controls suckers from the rootstock and promotes large, beautiful flowers. Unpruned plants become overgrown with small, poor-quality flowers. Use high-quality tools such as fine-tooth saws, sharp loppers, and sharp hand shears. Rose type dictates how, how often, and when to prune.

Roses need to be pruned in the spring, just before new growth begins. Prune after severe winter weather is past, usually in March.

To prune hybrid teas, floribundas, and grandifloras, remove all dead wood, thin stems, and diseased branches. Only strong, healthy branches should remain. Cut at a uniform height, leaving as much good wood as possible. Make angled cuts one-quarter inch above a strong outward-facing bud. This keeps the center of the bush open and lets more light into the center of the plant. Canes can be left as long as twenty-four to thirty inches, but after most winters they are pruned to twelve inches because of winter damage.

Some rose varieties with long stems will also need to be pruned in the fall so that their stems do not break off from the weight of winter snowfall. Remove spent blossom clusters or candelabras after the plant has gone dormant.

Use the following guidelines when pruning rosebushes:

- Prune higher for more flowers earlier, or prune lower for fewer, bigger flowers later.
- Remove weak and crossing canes.
- Cut back damaged, dead, or broken canes to healthy growth.
- Remove sucker growth below ground by cutting as close as possible to the root.

Severe winter damage may require vigorous pruning without regard for plant shaping. More severe pruning is done on hybrid teas to encourage longer stem length and larger blossoms. Longer canes, by contrast, produce shorter stems with

Pruning Roses

When pruning, remove weak or damaged canes.

Prune away spent blossoms.

Canes can be left as long as thirty inches but should be pruned to twelve inches after most winters.

After pruning, apply a sealer of white glue, silicone sealant, or pruning seal to ward off rose cane borers.

Cut down to the first set of five leaves when pruning spent blossoms.

smaller, more abundant blossoms. After pruning, apply a sealer of white glue, silicone sealant, or pruning seal to the cut to prevent rose cane borers from invading your bush. If larvae burrow into the stem, they will damage the plant.

Prune hardy climbing and rambler roses after flowering. Climbers bloom on old wood or last year's growth. If you cut out all the branches in the spring before the rose blooms, you will not get any blossoms. To prune, remove dead or diseased canes and take out old, weak canes. Don't let canes grow for more than three seasons, and don't let them get too crowded. Because many hybrid tea climbers and large-flowered ramblers are not vigorous, they are not pruned until the dormant season. Remove broken or diseased canes and those damaged by cold temperatures.

Prune climbing roses to make them fit the growing area. Training canes horizontally produces more flowers. Heading back long canes stimulates lateral growth for more blossoms and foliage.

Prune old-fashioned, or species, roses accord-ing to their bloom season. Prune single-season bloomers after they bloom. Cut long canes back by a third, and trim lateral canes back a few inches. Prune repeat bloomers to shape rather than cut-ting them back. Remove damaged canes, old canes as they lose vigor or become too crowded, and unwanted, misdirected growth.

Summer pruning to remove unwanted growth, suckers, weak or spindly shoots, and damaged canes improves rose quality. Pruning includes cut-ting flowers, which helps keep buds developing. Cutting flowers to the first five-leaflet leaf results in more vigorous growth. Leave at least two or more five-leaflet leaves between the cut and the main stem. On newly planted roses, remove only the flowers, leaving maximum leaf surface. Don't allow seed pods or rose hips to form until time for the plants to harden for winter.

FERTILIZING

Established roses benefit from fertilization. A good rule of thumb is to fertilize repeat-blooming roses in the spring right after pruning. Fertilize again when plants have developed flower buds and in August, or two months before the first fall frost. Older varieties that bloom only once are fertilized in the early spring. Rose fertilizers are available as dry formulations or liquids. Follow label directions for amounts. Organic fertilizers include steer manure, blood meal, bonemeal, or fish emulsion.

WINTER PROTECTION

Roses vary in their hardiness. Tree roses are the most tender, while some shrub roses are com-pletely hardy in all areas of Utah. Winter protec-tion lessens the effects of freezing and thawing. It also keeps branches from whipping in the wind, which can lead to loose roots.

Winter protection of some sort is needed where

Cosmos, salvia, and geraniums combine in a colorful display near the plaza fountain.

temperatures drop to twenty degrees below zero. Prune the spent flowers off the top of the canes. In high-wind areas, tie the canes together with twine. Form mulch mounds over the roses to prevent severe winter damage. Use soil, compost, wood chips, bark, or other material. Avoid straw that contains grain because it may attract mice that feed on the canes. Mound the mulch up over the top of the plant to protect the crown and bud areas. Colder winter temperatures require deeper mounds.

Some gardeners use Styrofoam cones, baskets, or other means to enclose their plants. In areas with extremely cold temperatures, remove climbers from their trellises, and cover them with mulch. Remove foliage from the plant and surrounding soil to reduce overwintering diseases. 🌹

Chapter 7

Tricks of the Trade

Here are a few tricks of the trade we've developed over the years to keep the gardens on Temple Square looking their best.

SOIL PREPARATION

It is difficult to find a good, true topsoil in the Salt Lake Valley, as mentioned in chapter 2. It is therefore particularly important to properly prepare soil for planting.

In many Temple Square gardens, including those on the Conference Center block, we use Utelite, which is then mixed with peat moss at a ratio of 50 percent Utelite and 50 percent peat moss before planting. A layer of two to three inches of mulch is then added to the top of the mixture after planting. Fertilizer, such as slow-release Osmocote, is also added because this mixture is sterile.

Utelite can also be added to heavy soils to help break them up and, because Utelite does not break down, to keep them aerated. Utelite retains as much as 12–35 percent of its weight in absorbed water and waterborne nutrients. Because it is sterile, it is free of diseases, weed seeds, and soilborne pests.

PURCHASING PLANTS

Avoid buying plants during or just after a cold spell. At such times, they are susceptible to damage from a freeze. In the Salt Lake Valley, the average last day for a frost is around Mother's Day in May. Tender annuals, such as begonias, should not be planted before then.

Look for plants that are free of weeds and moss growth, which indicates that they have been in their pots too long. Also, avoid buying plants that are wilted or have blotches on the leaves. Look for plants that are free of insects or insect

Adding Utelite and peat moss to soil can dramatically improve garden productivity.

damage, and check the soil, including around the roots, for insects. While you have the plant out of the pot or cell pack, check the roots to make sure they are not extremely root bound. Plants that show any of these stress factors are not usually healthy.

Try not to purchase your plants until you are

Root balls should look healthy when you remove them from the pack.

Root-bound plants often show signs of stress.

ready to plant. If you must store plants, keep them in a sheltered area away from the sun, wind, and fluctuating temperatures. Keep plants well watered without overwatering them.

PLANTING TIPS

Before you plant, prepare the bedding area. Dig the area to a depth of eight to ten inches. This allows plant roots to grow deep and better withstand the summer heat. Next, remove the plant from its container and gently loosen any compacted roots. If they will not loosen easily, it may help to water the soil surrounding the roots or to score the root ball.

When planting in hot weather, cut off plant blooms to reduce plant stress and help the roots establish more quickly. When the blooms are removed, the plant's energy will go to the root system instead of to the flowers.

MULCH

On Temple Square, we add a three-inch layer of mulch to all the flowerbeds when we finish planting the flowers in May. This helps to control the weeds and slows down moisture loss. Mulch also provides a finishing touch for the flower bed and makes it look neat and tidy. In the fall, incorporate this layer of mulch into the soil. This reduces the amount of fertilizer needed and creates an ideal environment for root growth. Mulch decomposes throughout the year and needs to be replaced each season.

It helps to understand the difference between mulch and compost. Both are organic, but mulch is chopped up plant materials that are not decomposed, while compost is the same material in a decomposed state. Organic material is vital to good garden soil. It improves drainage in clay soils and helps retain moisture and nutrients in sandy

Annual Seeds to Scatter in Fall

Annual poppy

Cosmos

Larkspur

Nigella

Alyssum

Verbena bonerenesis

Cleome

Bachelor's Button

Annual Seeds to Scatter in Spring

Candytuft

Cosmos

Alyssum

Zinnia

Nicotiana

Clarkia

Impatiens (tall varieties)

Cleome

soils. As organic material decomposes over time, it releases nutrients that plants need.

Digging raw wood chips, straw, or bark into the soil can deplete the soil of nitrogen. If you use these materials, you will have to add extra nitrogen. Ask your local nursery or county extension agent for more information.

SOWING SEEDS

Broadcasting or scattering seeds in and among your plants to self-germinate is one way to get more of a cottage garden look. Flowers such as poppies, cleome, and cornflowers do not transplant well but will do well broadcasted. Some seeds can be scattered in the fall, giving them a jump start in growth for the spring. Plants grown from seed are hardier and better adapted to climate fluctuations. On the other hand, using nursery-grown transplants gives you more control over the design of the garden. With transplants, you can choose the color, height, and placement of plants and immediately see your design.

A good rule of thumb is to plant seeds as deep as they are wide. Sprinkle seeds onto a soil surface that has already been prepared. Lightly rake the

area to mix seeds with the soil. Then gently tap the rake on the soil surface to make sure seeds and soil are in contact. You may want to place a marker in the area to remind you of what you have planted where, so that when your new seedlings come up, you will not mistake them for weeds.

As the seedlings emerge, thin them out as soon as they are large enough to handle. When thinning, leave the most vigorous seedlings and remove the smaller ones. Thinning can be done twice. Be careful not to disturb the roots of the remaining seedlings.

DEADHEADING

When a plant's blossoms fade and die back, the plant starts producing seeds. As the plant starts to produce seed, it will cut back on flower production. To prolong flower production, cut off the faded flowers. This process is called deadheading. It not only helps the garden look neat and tidy but also increases a plant's blooming time. When deadheading, follow the stem of the spent flower down to where it connects with the main stem and snip it off. When the plant has smaller flowers in mass groups, such as alyssum,

To deadhead 'Victoria Blue' salvia, follow the stem down to the first set of leaves and snip.

give it a light trim across the whole plant, trying not to remove more than one-third of the plant.

STAKING

The only time you need to tie up plants is when they become too top-heavy and bend down onto other flowers. If a plant seems as if it is going to break off or is disturbing other flowers, push a bamboo or metal stake into the ground by the crown of the plant. Be careful not to disturb the roots. Then use cotton string, natural jute, or cut-up pantyhose to tie the plant to the stake. Be sure to hide the stake and the string from sight. Don't tie the string too tight, and leave enough space for the plant to move freely. For plants like peonies, purchase circular plant hoops and push them into place before the plant gets too big. Then, as the plant grows, slide the circular hoop up to support the plants.

DIVIDING PERENNIALS

For spring-blooming perennials, it is best to divide them just after they have finished blooming or early in the fall. Likewise, summer and fall-blooming plants can be divided in early spring or after they have finished their bloom time. Never divide a plant just before it is ready to bloom because all of its energy is going toward reproduction rather than growth.

Consider the following guidelines when dividing your plants:

1. Do not divide a plant that in the spring has grown five inches or more.

2. Do not divide plants during hot, dry weather.

3. If possible, divide plants on a cool, cloudy day early in the spring.

4. Avoid late fall divisions because the new plant may not become established before frost sets in.

5. Soak plants thoroughly a few days before dividing.

6. To handle plants more easily, cut them back before dividing them in the fall.

7. Be sure the new planting spot has been well prepared before you divide a plant so that its roots will not dry out.

8. If you cannot plant immediately, the plant division can be potted and either shared with a friend or saved for future planting. Be sure to keep the pot watered.

EDGING

We keep the gardens at Temple Square as neat and tidy as possible. One of the ways we do this is by maintaining the edges of each area. Edges

1. *Trim back leaves before dividing perennials.*

2. *Dig out perennials with a pitchfork, and remove as much soil as possible.*

3. *Carefully break apart roots into sections.*

4. *Separate the sections into individual divisions for planting and share with neighbors.*

5. *Trim loose soil around newly planted sections and water thoroughly.*

6. *Replant healthy sections of plants at their previous soil levels.*

emphasize the lines in a garden. Lines visibly lead the eye around and through each area, enhancing appreciation for the garden.

We remove approximately two inches of soil along each sidewalk edge and push it up into the adjoining garden. This technique, called "shadow edging," makes the edges clean and keeps the soil from washing out onto the sidewalk.

In the areas between flowers and grass we use

Steel edging emphasizes the lines in a garden.

an eight-inch metal edging to keep the grass out of the flower beds. This edging must be deep because grass roots can grow under most types of edgings. Edgings need to go below six inches to keep grass roots in check.

CULTIVATING THE SOIL

After you have weeded and deadheaded your garden, be sure to go back with a narrow-bladed cultivator to fluff up the soil. Lightly rake the soil back and forth and remove any footprints. Compacted soil is not as attractive as fluffed-up soil, which will give your garden that just-worked-in look and make it sparkle.

WATERING TIPS

Most gardeners in the Salt Lake Valley overwater their plants. Plants do better with deep and infrequent watering, which keeps the roots moist deep within the soil. A layer of mulch two to three inches deep will help retain moisture.

Water is essential to plants. Newly planted plants require more water than established plants. Deep-rooted plants also require less water than shallow-rooted plants. It is best to know each plant's water requirements and to plant similar kinds of plants together. For example, plant low-water-use plants with other low-water-use plants.

Plants require as much oxygen as they do water. Overwatering deprives plants of oxygen and will kill them.

Do not forget to water plants in the winter when the weather has been dry. Even during cold weather plants need water. Pay special attention to plants under the eaves of the house that may not receive moisture from snowfall.

Check with your local extension agent to see how much water your lawn needs. Its moisture requirements change as the temperatures change.

TOOLS

Keep gardening tools in good condition. If maintained regularly, they can last for years. Major maintenance needs to be performed only once a year if tools are cared for correctly all year.

Once-a-year care includes sanding wooden handles to smooth out wood, oiling handles if necessary, repairing loose nails or screws, and sharpening blades as needed.

Year-round care includes cleaning soil off blades and tools. You can keep heavy clay soils from sticking to shovels or pitchforks by pushing them into a container of oily sand or gravel.

Oil tools several times a year, especially after each use. Cutting blades should be clean and dry before you oil them. Put oil on a clean rag and wipe blades and other metal parts. Regularly sharpen cutting-tool blades.

If wooden handles are worn, rough, or splintered, wrap them with insulating tape. Make sure the wood is dry so that the tape will stick properly. The tape should last for several weeks and can be replaced as needed.

Cold weather can freeze gasoline. Before storing gasoline-powered equipment, empty tanks. Check all cords on electrical tools for wear, and replace them if necessary.

Be sure to have some type of identifying mark on all your tools. Colored duct tape works well.

GENERAL MAINTENANCE

Remember that plants are not the only features in a garden. Do not forget benches, trellises, window boxes, greenhouses, frames, children's play equipment, fences, and so forth.

Hardwoods such as beech, mahogany, and teak are used in the construction of most of these gar-

den features. These woods are usually strong, long lasting, and durable. Such woods usually require little maintenance and are not prone to rotting.

Softwoods such as pine, fir, cedar, or spruce are also widely used, mostly because they cost less than hardwoods. But softwoods have a shorter lifespan and are more prone to damage. Regular treatment with a preservative is essential for these woods. Store items made of soft wood in a dry place in winter.

Cast iron is very heavy, making it ideal for containers that provide good stability. It is easy to paint with a brush or spray gun. Iron must be painted often to prevent rust.

Steel is often used in children's play equipment. Steel is strong and not easily damaged, but paint can easily peel off steel surfaces. Check steel products often and repaint as needed.

A stiff wire brush can be used for some cleaning jobs. It helps to remove rust, paint, algae, and other deposits on hard surfaces.

When maintaining wooden items, remove rotten areas with a chisel and fill with wood filler or putty. Smooth with a trowel. Replace missing nails with galvanized nails. Apply wood preservative to extend the life of wooden structures. 🌿

Chapter 8

Managing Pests and Disease

You can avoid problems with garden pests and diseases by giving your plants the right growing conditions. Properly prepare your soil, make sure you provide proper drainage, water your garden correctly, and place plants so that they receive the right amount of sun or shade. The following list of precautions can help you control problems with pests and diseases:

- Allow good air flow and spacing; don't crowd plants too closely together.
- Rotate flowers yearly.
- Remove weeds, dead flowers, fallen leaves, or other debris as soon as possible.
- Quickly remove and dispose of diseased plants.
- Select plant varieties that are pest and disease resistant.
- Water and fertilize as needed, but don't overwater.
- Water the soil, not the plants.

When a problem occurs, diagnose it properly before trying a solution. Familiarize yourself with the various options available to control problems. Start with the least disruptive solution and move on to harsher measures only when necessary. When you must use chemicals, read the instructions carefully and follow all directions. Certain chemicals can be toxic not only to pests but also to pets and people!

PEST MANAGEMENT

The pioneers did not leave insects behind when they headed west. One of the first serious

The Seagull Monument was built in honor of the miracle of seagulls eating Mormon crickets, which still plague areas of Utah.

encounters they had with an insect earned the pest the name Mormon cricket. A monument in the Temple Square gardens commemorates the miraculous intervention by seagulls on behalf of the early settlers.

Gardeners today fight the same pests that were

Powdery mildew on this lilac is a pathogenic disease caused by a living organism.

here a century and a half ago. While Mormon crickets have not attacked the gardens at Temple Square for some time, they still plague areas of the state each year. Fortunately, not all insects pose problems. Many pollinate plants or feed on pests. Most cause no harm, and only a few eat flowers, damage trees, or create other types of problems. Of the more than fifty thousand different insects in Utah, fewer than two hundred damage ornamental plants. Most of the other insects eat pests rather than plants.

Some insects damage ornamental plants and turf as they feed on and tunnel into leaves, roots, stems, seeds, and nuts. They carry disease and suck the sap from leaves, stems, roots, fruits, and flowers, which can damage, weaken, or kill plants. To successfully design an insect management program, you need to know insect classification, growth and development, and life cycles. Understanding insect life cycles will allow for intervention during the most vulnerable point in those cycles.

Signs of Insects and Mites

Scout your plantings carefully and regularly. The gardeners at Temple Square regularly check their plants for pests. Do the same in your garden and catch small outbreaks before they become serious problems.

Insect or mite pests may not be present or visible when you discover damage to your plants, but here are some common signs of their presence:

- Silk shelters, which usually do not enclose foliage. Caterpillars feed outside shelters and use them for protection from predators and weather.
- Web-enclosed foliage, with caterpillars feeding inside.
- Insect or mite remains such as eggshells, shed skins, cocoons, frass, and trails of silk.
- Scale and aphid coverings; most scale insects and some aphids excrete a protective waxy covering.
- Honeydew, which is a sticky liquid sugar excreted by insects; black sooty mold may grow on honeydew.
- Sawdust, wood chips, and pitch balls on or below trunks, created by bark beetles, wood borers, and shoot borers.

Pest Control Solutions

Plant pest infestations are similar to human illness. Successful treatment follows a sequence of controls.

Examine the site and the organisms, and compare your findings with the normal or healthy plant condition. If a plant shows signs of poor health or appears abnormal, identify and assess potential problems and their causes and severity. Remember that not all insects on plants are pests, so not all insects need to be controlled. Some are incidental; others are beneficial. On the other hand, some pests cause little damage at first but can cause serious problems later.

Determine a control prescription based on examination, identification, and assessment. Then choose either a preventive or curative method of insect control. You should take no action if infestations are not serious, if curative action may cause more harm than the infestation, or if curative timing is not appropriate. Consider a course of action consistent with the philosophy of Integrated Pest Management (IPM), which is a practical approach that when possible uses nonchemical controls to minimize pests.

Unfortunately, many people feel that insecticides are the only answer, and, as a result, they overuse them. Never apply insecticides unless pests are causing damage. Do not apply insecticides in high dosages, on a calendar basis, or simply whenever insects appear. Apply them only if they are the best control, and make sure you choose the best chemical and application method. Consult labels, distributors, or your local extension service for control information and proper prescription.

Integrated Pest Management

The theory behind Integrated Pest Management is that several techniques are necessary for successful levels of pest control. IPM techniques are used in a coordinated manner so that all costs—social, environmental, and monetary—are considered. This is important at the gardens on Temple Square because continual public access and traffic make it quite difficult to spray or apply insecticides.

The following guidelines are part of IPM:

- The basis of pest management is the maintenance of plant health through good prevention. Healthy, vigorous plants better tolerate and often avoid pest problems.

Because of public access and traffic, insecticides are not used on Temple Square. Many people mistakenly believe that insecticides are the only answer to pest control.

- Various techniques, including cultural controls, sanitation, pesticides, and other appropriate measures are used in coordinated ways to manage pests.
- Monitoring determines the need for pest control by detecting changes in pest populations.
- IPM techniques try to manage pests at acceptable levels rather than to eliminate them. Some damage is tolerable as long as the threatened damage does not exceed the cost to control the pest. In Temple Square landscape plantings, we determine what constitutes a damaging level of pest injury by assessing aesthetic considerations and monetary costs. "Insurance" applications of pesticides are not compatible with IPM. The only time we use preventive applications is when the potential for pest injury is predictable and when options will not exist after an infestation occurs.

METHODS OF INSECT CONTROL

Each method of insect control has advantages and disadvantages. Here are some ways we manage insect pests at the gardens on Temple Square.

Cultural Controls

Methods of cultural control are aimed more at prevention than cure. If plants are healthy, they can better tolerate injuries from pests.

- Plant the right plant in the right place, and modify soil conditions as needed.
- Vary planting times, and use good irrigation and fertilizing practices.
- Give plants adequate space, and avoid excessive watering to suppress root rot.
- To suppress or prevent infestations, consider altering pest environment or influencing pest behavior. Creating an unfavorable environment for pests is a growing practice.

Knowing the signs and symptoms of disease, such as root rot in the geraniums above, is essential for accurate diagnosis.

- To kill harmful pests or slow their reproduction, change the environment during the most vulnerable part of their life cycle, which is usually just after they hatch. Knowing a pest's life cycle is an essential element of cultural control.

Resistance

Pest- and disease-resistant plants are developed through breeding, selection, and genetic engineering. Total immunity is rare, but resistant varieties thrive despite pests. For example, we select mildew-resistant roses, phlox, and zinnias for Temple Square gardens.

Sanitation

To reduce pests, remove them, their shelter, and their food, including unhealthy plant tissue. Weed out inferior and diseased plants. Keeping your garden free of dead plant material helps control disease. Remove weeds and plants that host viruses or insect pests.

Mechanical Controls

Mechanical controls reduce pests by handpicking and trapping, or by using insect screens, barriers, sticky bands, and shading devices. Mechanical controls require time and labor and may be impractical on a large scale. Avoid bruising plants during handling to prevent injuries and reduce infections.

Pheromone traps contain synthetic female sex attractants (pheromones) that have been identified and developed as lures for male insects. Light traps or "bug-zappers" are popular, but research shows that they do not control insect pests. Most insects caught in the traps are beneficial or harmless. These light sources also attract insects from surrounding areas.

Legal Controls

Quarantines restrict movement of potential pests into an area, or they use public resources to eradicate, prevent, or control pests. Pests may also be kept out of an area through careful monitoring of plant introductions. Buy your nursery stock from reputable sources to avoid introducing unwanted pests to your garden.

Natural Controls

In a balanced ecosystem, natural enemies control pests. Pest outbreaks occur when natural controls fail. Typical nonpathogenic (or natural) controls are high winds, rain, extreme heat, or freezing temperatures. Cold, wet weather, for example, helps control pests such as spider mites or grasshoppers.

Plants also offer effective controls. Gums or resins produced by trees can push insects out of tree wounds, where they feed. Leaves and needles can be toxic to pests, and leaf coatings can prevent disease infections.

Biological Controls

The best controls for many pests are antagonistic insects and diseases, including parasites, predators, or pathogenic organisms that feed on or damage pests. They can be found naturally in the ecosystem, or they can be humanly introduced. Under ideal conditions, they become established in the environment and provide long-term pest control. Environmental factors such as dust, unfavorable weather, biological competitors, and pesticides, however, may diminish their effectiveness.

Parasitic nematodes are biological insect controls that invade and kill susceptible insects. They need moist conditions and are useful in control-

Slugs and snails leave behind telltale signs of chewed holes in leaves and stems.

Check your plants regularly for pests so you can avoid mite damage to your marigolds and other flowers.

ling white grubs, billbugs, sod webworms, root weevils, and crown borers.

The advantages of biological controls include permanence, safety, and economy. Once established, these controls are relatively safe with no hazardous toxicity or environmental pollution.

Introducing biological controls in small isolated landscapes is usually not effective.

Reproductive Controls

Reproductive controls reduce pests by physical treatments or substances that cause sterility, alter sexual behavior, or otherwise disrupt normal reproduction. They are not used on small-scale landscapes.

Chemical Controls

Using chemicals to reduce insect populations by poisoning, attracting, or repelling insects is still the most common pest-management tool. Chemicals are highly effective and economical, and they offer quick, short-term control if used correctly. When pest populations cause significant plant damage despite natural controls, pesticide applications can offer the best solution.

Chemicals can control multiple species of pests with a single application, which is an advantage of using insecticides in ornamental ecosystems. One application, for example, can control caterpillars and aphids feeding on the same plant.

Apply chemicals when pests are most vulnerable, usually when they are young. For example, scale insects should be controlled in the crawler stage before they develop waxy coverings. Apply chemicals where the pest spends most of its time. For example, spray the undersides of leaves to control white flies.

Many insect and mite species go through multiple generations in a single season. Unless the population is controlled in earlier generations, pests can increase to damaging levels as the season progresses. Most insecticides last only one to four weeks and must be reapplied to control later generations.

Sometimes it is necessary to apply pesticide spray to prevent serious problems in the Temple Square gardens. We try to use pesticides that target only the offending pest and that are least likely to kill natural predators or other beneficial insects. These biorational pesticides should be used only when needed.

Bacillus thuringiensis, or Bt, is a bacterial disease organism manufactured and sold as a "microbial insecticide" under trade names such as Dipel, Thuricide, and Javelin. Bt is considered nontoxic to humans, pets, and wildlife. It is exempt from food-crop tolerance standards and can be used until crops are harvested. Bt is highly specific, and most formulations only affect leaf and needle-feeding caterpillars. It is a stomach poison that must be ingested to be effective. It does not affect predators, parasites, and insect pollinators.

Oils for Insect and Mite Control

Pest-control oils are highly refined, specialty sprays with impurities that can damage plants. Oils suffocate insects and mites by clogging their breathing holes. Dormant oils are often used as sprays to control scales, aphids, or mites that overwinter on woody plants.

Apply dormant oils on warm spring days before buds break. Thorough coverage is essential for effective control. Oils are easy to use and have a low risk for gardeners, and they are relatively safe for predators and parasites as well.

Use oils cautiously because they may injure some plants and trees. Black walnut, some maples, Russian olive, junipers, and redbud are oil-sensitive. Blue spruce tolerates treatment but loses the waxy bloom that gives it its distinctive color. Always use oils according to label instructions.

Soaps for Insect and Mite Control

Environmental awareness is increasing the use of soaps as insecticides/miticides. Soaps control most small, soft-bodied insects and mites like aphids, thrips, psylla, and spider mites, as well as larger insects like honey locust plant bugs and pear slugs.

Insecticidal soaps have several advantages. They are safe and easy to mix and apply. Their insecticidal activity is specifically targeted so that most beneficial insects, parasites, and predators are not adversely affected. Likewise, birds, pets, and wildlife are not injured by treatments.

Insecticidal soaps can damage some plants. If their use on a specific plant is not known, test them first by spraying them on the plant and waiting a day to see if they cause leaf burn. Soaps are strictly contact insecticides with no residual activity, so apply them thoroughly.

SLUG AND SNAIL CONTROL

The worst pests faced by the Temple Square gardens, like many gardens throughout the country, are slugs and snails rather than insects. These creatures are mollusks. They are active at night, chewing holes in leaves or stems. The damage they cause can be confused with damage done by feeding caterpillars. Caterpillars leave large droppings on plant foliage, while slugs leave shiny streaks of dried slime on plants and soil. Caterpillars may leave part of the leaf veins and stems untouched, but slugs chew through leaves and stems.

Mulches, boards, or rocks provide cool, moist environments in which snails and slugs can hide and lay eggs in clusters of twenty to one hundred. At 50 degrees, eggs hatch in less than ten days and mature in three months to a year. Offspring are smaller and lighter colored but resemble adults.

Because gardeners water frequently, space

Slugs and snails are the worst pests faced by Temple Square gardeners.

their plants close together, and use mulches, often snails and slugs thrive in gardens. To control these pests, carefully inspect imported plants, eliminate weeds, reduce watering, and clean up debris piles and other hiding places. Apply molluskicides (snail bait) as needed, and regularly go on patrol to hunt them down.

One of the best methods of ridding your garden of snails is to pick them up, put them in a plastic bag, and throw them away. Do not smash snails on the sidewalk or in your garden as you may only be spreading their eggs. One snail left in your garden can produce as many as three hundred eggs!

The fall is a great time to hand pick snails after summer annuals have been removed. To help in the control, you may also spread molluskicides.

PLANT DISEASES

A disease is a process rather than a condition. In gardening, a disease is anything that interferes with normal plant function. It can be a biotic or pathogenic infection caused by living organisms, or it can be an abiotic or nonpathogenic, physiological disorder. Powdery mildew is a pathogenic disease caused by a living organism. Iron deficiency is a nonpathogenic disease caused by a physiological disorder.

Nonpathogenic Diseases

Most plant diseases (about 80 percent of landscape problems) can be attributed to nonpathogenic disorders. These are noninfectious diseases that do not move from diseased to healthy plants and cannot be stopped by pesticides. These nonpathogenic, physiological disorders result from unfavorable weather, mechanical damage, improper watering, nutrient deficiencies, excess salts, or toxic chemicals.

Pathogenic Diseases

Pathogens cause infectious diseases by growing in plant tissue and disrupting normal physiological functions. As pathogenic organisms grow, they spread to other plants, causing disease outbreaks. Disease management reduces or delays epidemics enough to let plants thrive.

Discard all bulbs that develop mold.

Infectious diseases need three conditions to develop:
- A pathogenic organism.
- Available, susceptible host plants.
- Favorable environmental conditions.

Once an infectious disease starts, it grows until the pathogenic organism or host plant is removed or until environmental conditions stop development of the disease. Pesticides are designed to stop pathogen growth on or within host plants and to protect healthy plants. For many pathogens, however, no chemical treatment is available.

Pathogenic Organisms

Fungi, bacteria, and viruses cause most infectious plant diseases. Parasitic seed plants, including dodder and mistletoe, also attack some plants.

Fungi, which are responsible for most plant diseases, get their nutrients from plants and animals. Fungi that attack live plants are called parasites.

Fungi develop fine, string-like filaments that mechanically or chemically penetrate plant surfaces. Injuries or natural openings in plant surfaces often increase the severity of disease caused by fungi.

Fungi produce spores that function like seeds. These spores are dispersed by wind, water, equipment, insects, or plant seeds. Each spore can germinate and cause more infections. Some fungi survive months or years as resting spores in soil or plant debris.

Bacteria, the second most important class of plant pathogens, are single-celled organisms that reproduce by division. They generally enter host plants through injuries or natural openings. A common sign of bacterial disease is a viscous, slimy mass of live and dead bacteria from oozing, infected tissues.

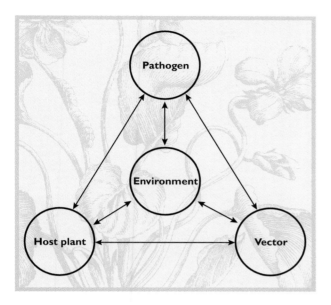

Infectious Disease Development Chart

proving hostile to another disease. Moisture extremes also influence disease development. Fungi and bacteria are favored by wet conditions that enhance spore production and release. Rose rust is favored by high humidity, while leaf spot in aspen and fire blight in pears require moisture from dripping dews or splashing rains in order to spread. Other factors, such as light, wind, pH, fertility, and soil type, also influence disease development.

Recognizing Plant Diseases

The distribution of diseased plants within an area provides valuable information for diagnosis. In the early stages, infectious diseases usually affect scattered plants or small clusters rather than large areas. Diseases that occur suddenly and affect many different plants are more likely to be noninfectious diseases. To identify diseases correctly, carefully observe the disease symptoms and the signs of the pathogen. Knowing characteristic signs and symptoms of disease is essential for accurate diagnosis, which is the first step in controlling disease.

Signs are identifiable structures of the pathogen that occur with the disease. These include fungal spores, spore-producing bodies, bacterial ooze, and parts of parasitic plants. A magnifying lens or microscope can help identify these.

Symptoms are the plant's reaction to sickness or injury. They appear as tissue overdevelopment, including swelling of plant tissue; tissue underdevelopment, including lack of chlorophyll and stunted growth of plant parts; and tissue death, including leaf or flower blights, leaf spots, root rots, cankers, and wilting.

Viruses are so small that they can only be seen with an electron microscope. Viruses cannot use organic chemicals by themselves. They reproduce by taking over host plant cells and directing the cells to replicate new viruses, causing plant disease.

Since viruses are inactive outside the host cells, they cannot penetrate intact host surfaces. They enter through injuries caused by insects or man, and through tubers or grafts. Because viruses are so small, viral diseases are identified in plants by the symptoms they exhibit.

Parasites can be stopped with pesticides, which reduce the susceptibility of the host plant and make conditions unfavorable for parasites to develop. They do so without changing the conditions favorable to the host plant.

Temperatures may favor one disease while

Chapter 9

Favorite Lists

A splendid garden needs a mix of perennials, annuals, bulbs, grasses, and shrubs, choreographed to create a dazzling year-round display.

The beauty of perennials is that they return year after year as mainstays of your garden. The wide diversity of available perennials allows you to select plants that will exactly fit your garden. Annuals, which complete their life cycle in a year or less, create versatility in the garden. Available in every hue and shade imaginable, they provide instant color to quickly transform the look of your garden. Bulbs lay dormant beneath the ground for much of the year, waiting patiently for their turn to take center stage with an incredible array of color. Grasses and shrubs provide form, texture, and stability.

The following lists are not intended to be comprehensive, but they reflect some of our favorite plants from the gardens at Temple Square. The detailed descriptions tell you what we have learned about the plant and how it has performed. The lists may help you select a plant for a specific site or a particular bloom season. The lists may also spark ideas for plants to try in your garden.

The descriptive sections are organized in an easy-reference format. Each entry begins with the plant's botanical name, followed by its common name. Some entries refer to a number of species and hybrids, such as Hosta, while other entries refer to a single species, such as Coreopsis *grandiflora* and Coreopsis *verticillata*. We offer detailed descriptions in our lists of favorite:

- Perennials
- Annuals
- Bulbs
- Roses
- Grasses
- Trees and Shrubs

We also provide basic, at-a-glance information in our lists of favorite:

- Easy-care perennials
- Long-blooming perennials
- Perennials that do not require deadheading
- Summer and autumn perennials to cut back before blooming
- Shade-loving plants
- Plants for dry, hot gardens

As you review the lists, remember that some of the perennials that are hardy in the gardens at Temple Square may not do as well in a home garden with the same USDA hardiness zone rating. This may occur for several reasons. At Temple Square, many of the gardens are located on rooftops where heating pipes run underneath the flower beds. Also, many of the gardens are surrounded by buildings that absorb solar radiation and make the area warmer. Not all plants will grow successfully in one location, so evaluate growing conditions and match a plant as closely as possible with the environment in which it will live. ❧

Favorite

Perennials

Achillea

CULTIVAR: 'Moonshine'
COMMON NAME: Yarrow
COLOR: Light yellow
HEIGHT: 2 feet
WIDTH: 2 feet
LIGHT: Full sun
HARDINESS: Zones 3–8
FLOWERING SEASON: June–Sept.

This perennial is long blooming, tolerant of dry soil, and good for hot areas. In wet soil, it is susceptible to root rot.

Achillea millefolium

COMMON NAME: Yarrow
COLOR: Variety
HEIGHT: 3–4 feet
WIDTH: 3 feet
LIGHT: Full sun
HARDINESS: Zones 3–9
FLOWERING SEASON: June–Aug.

Yarrow is a great cut flower, but it can be invasive. Its basal foliage holds its form over winter.

Achillea tomentosa

CULTIVAR: 'Aurea'
COMMON NAME: Woolly Yarrow
COLOR: Lemon yellow
HEIGHT: 8 inches
WIDTH: 18 inches
LIGHT: Full sun
HARDINESS: Zones 3–9
FLOWERING SEASON: June–Sept.

This is an easy-care, mat-forming compact plant. Use it in rock walls or as ground cover in sunny areas.

Aconitum napellus

COMMON NAME: Monkshood
COLOR: Indigo blue, mauve, white
HEIGHT: 3–4 feet
WIDTH: 12–18 inches
LIGHT: Partial shade
HARDINESS: Zones 3–7
FLOWERING SEASON: July–Aug.

All parts of this easy-care plant are poisonous. It may need to be staked, but it can be cut back in early June to control its height. It does not like tree root competition. After being planted, it should be left alone for many years so it can establish itself.

Ajuga

COMMON NAME: Bugleweed
COLOR: Blue, pink, white
HEIGHT: 6–9 inches
WIDTH: 24 inches
LIGHT: Partial shade–full sun
HARDINESS: Zones 4–9
FLOWERING SEASON: May–June

Bugleweed is an easy-care plant that offers good ground cover. It can become invasive but is not difficult to control. Thin the plants occasionally to prevent overcrowding and to invigorate them.

Alcea (Althaea) rosea

CULTIVAR: 'Singles'
COMMON NAME: Hollyhock
COLOR: Yellow, pink, purple, white
HEIGHT: 5–8 feet
WIDTH: 24 inches
LIGHT: Full sun
HARDINESS: Zones 3–8
FLOWERING SEASON: June–Aug.

It is better to let this biennial reseed than to pull up old plants. It can develop rust, leaf spot, and spider mites, and may require application of an insecticidal soap.

Alchemilla mollis

COMMON NAME: Lady's Mantle
COLOR: Greenish yellow
HEIGHT: 15–18 inches
WIDTH: 24–30 inches
LIGHT: Partial shade–full sun
HARDINESS: Zones 4–8
FLOWERING SEASON: June–Sept.

Cut back lady's mantle after blooming to promote a new flush of leaves. It self-seeds but is not invasive. Divide it in the spring.

Anemone x hybrida

CULTIVAR: 'Honorine Jobert'
COMMON NAME: Japanese Anemone
COLOR: White
HEIGHT: 4–5 feet
WIDTH: 18 inches
LIGHT: Partial shade–full sun
HARDINESS: Zones 4–8
FLOWERING SEASON: Aug.–Sept.

This perennial does not like drought. It can be invasive but is easily controlled.

Anemone japonica

CULTIVAR: 'September Charm'
COMMON NAME: Japanese Anemone
COLOR: Mauve
HEIGHT: 4–5 feet
WIDTH: 18 inches
LIGHT: Partial shade–full sun
HARDINESS: Zones 5–9
FLOWERING SEASON: Aug.–Sept.

This perennial does not do well in drought conditions. It can be invasive, but it is not difficult to control and is generally considered an easy-care plant.

Anemone sylvestris

COMMON NAME: Snowdrop Anemone
COLOR: White
HEIGHT: 12–18 inches
WIDTH: 12 inches
LIGHT: Partial shade–full sun,
   especially in afternoon
HARDINESS: Zones 5–9
FLOWERING SEASON: May–June

Snowdrop anemone can be invasive, but it is easily controlled by weeding. It spreads through root suckers and should be thinned after flowering.

Aquilegia

CULTIVAR: 'McKana Hybrids'
COMMON NAME: Columbine
COLOR: Blue, yellow, red
HEIGHT: 30 inches
WIDTH: 24 inches
LIGHT: Partial shade–full sun
HARDINESS: Zones 3–8
FLOWERING SEASON: May–June,
   possibly July

This plant does not like the hot afternoon sun, and it can develop crown rot in heavy soil. It has a life span of only three to four years but is an easy-care plant. Cut it back after it flowers.

Arabis caucasica

COMMON NAME: Rock Cress
COLOR: White
HEIGHT: 12 inches
WIDTH: 18 inches
LIGHT: Full sun
HARDINESS: Zones 4–7
FLOWERING SEASON: April–May

This easy-care perennial tolerates hot, dry conditions. For full plants, cut them back by half after they flower, and divide them every three years after they flower. Dead and yellowing leaves need to be removed in the summer.

Arenaria montana

COMMON NAME: Mountain Sandwort
COLOR: White
HEIGHT: ½ inch
WIDTH: 12 inches or more
LIGHT: Partial shade–full sun,
   especially in afternoon
HARDINESS: Zones 4–7
FLOWERING SEASON: May–June

This compact plant is good for rock gardens. It has grayish green leaves and a shallow root system. Water it often during dry spells.

Armeria maritima

COMMON NAME: Sea Thrift
COLOR: Pink, white
HEIGHT: 12 inches
WIDTH: 12 inches
LIGHT: Full sun
HARDINESS: Zones 3–9
FLOWERING SEASON: May–June

This is a good easy-care plant for rock gardens. It performs well in poor, dry soil. It has grass-like mounded foliage. Divide when mounds open or it will rot in the center. Because this is hard to do successfully, it's best to replace the plant.

Artemisia schmidtiana

CULTIVAR: 'Silvermound'
COMMON NAME: Wormwood
COLOR: Yellow
HEIGHT: 12 inches
WIDTH: 18 inches
LIGHT: Full sun
HARDINESS: Zones 3–7
FLOWERING SEASON: Aug.–Sept.

This plant is grown for its gray aromatic foliage. It is drought tolerant but will die in heavy, poorly drained soils. Some varieties can become invasive. Cut off insignificant flower heads.

Aruncus dioicus

COMMON NAME: Goatsbeard
COLOR: White, cream
HEIGHT: 4–6 feet
WIDTH: 4 feet
LIGHT: Partial–full shade
HARDINESS: Zones 6–9
FLOWERING SEASON: July–Sept.

Goatsbeard has plume-like flowers with fern-like leaves. Deadhead faded flowers or leave them on for winter interest.

Asarum europaeum

COMMON NAME: Wild Ginger
COLOR: Dark green leaves
HEIGHT: To 6 inches
WIDTH: 12 feet
LIGHT: Partial–full shade
HARDINESS: Zones 4–8
FLOWERING SEASON: May–June

Wild ginger offers great ground cover. It is grown for its foliage rather than its insignificant flowers.

Asclepias tuberosa

COMMON NAME: Butterfly Weed
COLOR: Orange, red, yellow
HEIGHT: 2–3 feet
WIDTH: 2 feet
LIGHT: Full sun
HARDINESS: Zones 4–9
FLOWERING SEASON: July–Sept.

This plant tolerates poor, dry soil, and is good for hot areas. Deadheading prolongs its bloom time. Allow its second blossoms to mature into ornamental fruit, and cut it back in the spring.

Aster frikartii

CULTIVAR: 'Mönch'
COMMON NAME: Aster
COLOR: Violet blue
HEIGHT: 28 inches
WIDTH: 16 inches
LIGHT: Full sun
HARDINESS: Zones 5–8
FLOWERING SEASON: July–Sept.

This easy-care plant has long-lasting flowers. Cutting it back in May yields stronger flower stems but may delay bloom time.

Aster novi-belgii

CULTIVAR: 'Ada Ballard'
COMMON NAME: Michaelmas Daisy
COLOR: Variety
HEIGHT: 4 feet
WIDTH: 3 feet
LIGHT: Partial shade–full sun
HARDINESS: Zones 4–8
FLOWERING SEASON: Sept.–Oct.

Divide asters every year or two in the spring to keep them vigorous and to control their spread. Cut them back in June and August for more compact plants. If you don't prune them in early summer, you'll need to stake them.

Astilbe x arendsii

COMMON NAME: Astilbe
COLOR: Pink, red, white, peach
HEIGHT: 2–4 feet
WIDTH: 2 feet
LIGHT: Partial–full shade
HARDINESS: Zones 4–8
FLOWERING SEASON: June–Sept.

This perennial does not like clay or alkaline soil, especially when the soil is dry. Give it a high-nitrogen fertilizer. It needs no deadheading, and its dried seed heads create winter interest.

Aubrieta

COMMON NAME: False Rock Cress
COLOR: Rose, purple
HEIGHT: 6 inches
WIDTH: 24 inches
LIGHT: Partial shade–full sun, especially in afternoon
HARDINESS: Zones 4–8
FLOWERING SEASON: April–May

Aubrieta forms a spreading mat of flowers. It is a good marker plant for tulips but has a short life. Cut it back after flowering.

Aurinia saxatilis

CULTIVAR: 'Citrina,' 'Alyssum'
COMMON NAME: Basket-of-Gold
COLOR: Pale yellow
HEIGHT: 8 inches
WIDTH: 10 inches
LIGHT: Full sun
HARDINESS: Zones 3–7
FLOWERING SEASON: April–May

Basket-of-gold, with its spreading gray-green foliage, works well in rock gardens. Cut it back after it flowers.

Aurinia saxatilis

CULTIVAR: 'Gold Dust'
COMMON NAME: Basket-of-Gold, Alyssum
COLOR: Bright yellow
HEIGHT: 8–10 inches
WIDTH: 18 inches
LIGHT: Full sun
HARDINESS: Zones 3–7
FLOWERING SEASON: April–May

'Alyssum,' with its spreading gray-green foliage, works well in rock gardens. Cut it back after it flowers.

Baptisia australis

COMMON NAME: False Indigo, Wild Blue Indigo
COLOR: Dark blue, sometimes flecked with white
HEIGHT: 5 feet
WIDTH: 24 inches
LIGHT: Partial shade–full sun
HARDINESS: Zones 3–9
FLOWERING SEASON: June

This drought-tolerant, slow-growing plant does not need deadheading but may need staking.

Bellis perennis

CULTIVAR: 'Pomponette'
COMMON NAME: English Daisy
COLOR: White, pink, crimson
HEIGHT: 2–8 inches
WIDTH: 2–8 inches
LIGHT: Partial shade–full sun, especially in afternoon
HARDINESS: Zones 6–10
FLOWERING SEASON: March–June

This biennial makes a great companion plant for spring-flowering bulbs. Deadhead it regularly to prolong bloom time and give it a light mulch.

Bergenia cordifolia

COMMON NAME: Elephant's Ears
COLOR: Pink, red, white, salmon
HEIGHT: 12 inches
WIDTH: 18 inches
LIGHT: Partial shade–full sun
HARDINESS: Zones 3–8
FLOWERING SEASON: May–June

This evergreen perennial produces good cut flowers. Use it in mass plantings. It is an easy-care plant that spreads by rhizomes. Divide it every four years.

Boltonia asteroides

CULTIVAR: 'Snowbank'
COMMON NAME: Snowbank Boltonia
COLOR: White, lilac, purple
HEIGHT: 5 feet
WIDTH: 3 feet
LIGHT: Partial shade–full sun
HARDINESS: Zones 4–9
FLOWERING SEASON: Sept.–Oct.

This is a low-maintenance, drought-tolerant plant that needs no dead-heading and can stand heat and humidity. Divide it in the spring or fall every three to five years.

Brunnera macrophylla

COMMON NAME: Siberian Bugloss
COLOR: Blue
HEIGHT: 12 inches
WIDTH: 24 inches
LIGHT: Partial shade–full sun, especially in afternoon
HARDINESS: Zones 3–8
FLOWERING SEASON: May–June

This is a good bulb-companion plant with flowers similar to forget-me-nots. It's also an easy-care plant that reseeds freely but not invasively. Cut it back after it flowers.

Campanula carpatica

CULTIVAR: 'Blue & White Clips'
COMMON NAME: Carpathian Harebell
COLOR: Blue, white
HEIGHT: 6–12 inches
WIDTH: 12–24 inches
LIGHT: Partial shade–full sun
HARDINESS: Zones 3–8
FLOWERING SEASON: June–Sept.

This is a good plant for rock gardens. It does not like heat or high humidity and has a short life. Divide it every two years. It attracts slugs and snails but is generally an easy-care plant.

Campanula persicifolia

COMMON NAME: Peach-leaved Bellflower
COLOR: Lilac, blue, white
HEIGHT: 24–36 inches
WIDTH: 12 inches
LIGHT: Partial shade–partial sun
HARDINESS: Zones 3–6
FLOWERING SEASON: June–Aug.

This easy-care, long-blooming plant produces good cut flowers. Its delicate blossom colors are best preserved in shade. Cut back faded flower stalks to promote flowering after July.

Campanula portenschlagiana

COMMON NAME: Dalmatian Bellflower
COLOR: Blue, deep purple
HEIGHT: 4–6 inches
WIDTH: 20 inches
LIGHT: Partial shade–partial sun
HARDINESS: Zones 4–8
FLOWERING SEASON: June–Aug.

This easy-care plant is good for rock gardens. It produces star-shaped flowers above creeping foliage.

Campanula poscharskyana

COMMON NAME: Serbian Bellflower
COLOR: Blue
HEIGHT: 6 inches
WIDTH: 24 inches
LIGHT: Partial shade–partial sun
HARDINESS: Zones 4–7
FLOWERING SEASON: June–Sept.

This vigorous perennial is an easy-care plant that spreads by underground runners.

Campanula pyramidalis

COMMON NAME: Chimney Bellflower
COLOR: Light blue, white
HEIGHT: 8 feet
WIDTH: 24 inches
LIGHT: Partial shade–full sun
HARDINESS: Zones 6–8
FLOWERING SEASON: June–Aug.

This is an easy-care, short-lived plant that produces fragrant flowers and is best grown as a biennial.

Centranthus ruber

COMMON NAME: Jupiter's Beard, Red Valerian, Keys of Heaven
COLOR: White, light pink, dark crimson
HEIGHT: 3 feet
WIDTH: 3 feet
LIGHT: Full sun
HARDINESS: Zones 4–9
FLOWERING SEASON: June–Aug.

This is an easy-care plant that tolerates hot, dry conditions. Deadheading will prolong bloom time. If you cut it down after blooming, it will rebloom in the fall.

Chrysanthemum x morifolium, syn. Dendranthema x grandiflorum)

CULTIVAR: 'Clara Curtis'
COLOR: Variety
HEIGHT: 10–30 inches
WIDTH: 10–30 inches
LIGHT: Full sun
HARDINESS: Zones 5–10
FLOWERING SEASON: Aug.–Oct.

Cut and pinch back this perennial to produce compact plants. Doing so after June, however, may discourage bloom. Discontinue fertilizing by the end of July.

Cimicifuga racemosa

COMMON NAME: Black Snakeroot, Black Cohosh
COLOR: White
HEIGHT: 4–7 feet
WIDTH: 24 inches
LIGHT: Partial shade
HARDINESS: Zones 3–8
FLOWERING SEASON: July–Aug.

This easy-care perennial has dark brown-purple foliage. It is a fall-blooming plant with fragrant, bottlebrush-like flowers. It needs no deadheading.

Cimicifuga simplex

CULTIVAR: 'Brunette'
COMMON NAME: Autumn Snakeroot
COLOR: White
HEIGHT: 4–7 feet
WIDTH: 24 inches
LIGHT: Partial shade
HARDINESS: Zones 3–8
FLOWERING SEASON: September–frost

This easy-care perennial has dark brown-purple foliage. It is a fall-blooming plant with fragrant, bottlebrush-like flowers. It needs no deadheading.

Clematis jackmanii

COMMON NAME: Clematis
COLOR: Purple
HEIGHT: 6–9 feet
WIDTH: 24 inches
LIGHT: Partial shade
HARDINESS: Zones 4–8
FLOWERING SEASON: July–Sept.

Clematis is a late-blooming, large-flowered climber that bears flowers on the current year's shoots and needs no deadheading. Locate the roots and crown in a shady spot. When pruning, cut back all previous year's stems to a pair of strong buds six to eight inches above soil level.

Doronicum cordatum

COMMON NAME: Leopard's Bane
COLOR: Yellow
HEIGHT: 18–24 inches
WIDTH: 12–18 inches
LIGHT: Partial shade
HARDINESS: Zones 3–8
FLOWERING SEASON: May–July

This plant produces daisy-like flowers that are good for cutting. It can reseed nicely and may go completely dormant after blooming. It does not tolerate drought but is generally an easy-care plant.

Echinacea purpurea

COMMON NAME: Coneflower
COLOR: Purple, white, pink
HEIGHT: 2–4 feet
WIDTH: 2 feet
LIGHT: Partial shade–full sun
HARDINESS: Zones 3–8
FLOWERING SEASON: July–Sept.

Coneflower is a long-blooming plant that reseeds readily if spent blossoms are not removed. Light shade will enhance its color. It is an easy-care plant that resists drought and heat.

Epimedium alpinum

COMMON NAME: Alpine Barrenwort
COLOR: Red, yellow
HEIGHT: 12 inches
WIDTH: 12 inches
LIGHT: Partial–full shade
HARDINESS: Zones 4–8
FLOWERING SEASON: May–June

This perennial can be grown as a ground cover. It produces dainty, airy flowers. Once it becomes established, it does well in dry shade and can compete with tree roots.

Filipendula rubra

COMMON NAME: Queen-of-the-prairie
COLOR: Peach–pink
HEIGHT: 6 feet
WIDTH: 3 feet
LIGHT: Partial shade–full sun
HARDINESS: Zones 3–8
FLOWERING SEASON: May–June

This plant has red stems and produces a fluffy plume-type flower with fragrant blooms. It needs no deadheading.

Gaillardia x grandiflora

CULTIVAR: 'Burgundy'
COMMON NAME: Blanket Flower
COLOR: Burgundy, wine, red, yellow
HEIGHT: 2–3 feet
WIDTH: 2 feet
LIGHT: Full sun
HARDINESS: Zones 2–10
FLOWERING SEASON: June–frost

This easy-care plant is drought and heat tolerant, but it often succumbs to wet overwintering conditions. Deadhead it regularly, and stake the tall varieties. 'Goblin' is a short variety that does not need staking.

Galium odoratum

COMMON NAME: Sweet Woodruff
COLOR: White
HEIGHT: 4–6 inches
WIDTH: Ground cover
LIGHT: Partial shade
HARDINESS: Zones 4–8
FLOWERING SEASON: May–June

This easy-care plant provides good ground cover for shady areas. Its tiny white flowers are sometimes fragrant. It can be invasive but is easily controlled.

Gaura lindheimeri

CULTIVAR: 'Whirling Butterflies,' 'Siskiyou Pink'
COMMON NAME: Apple Blossom Grass
COLOR: White, pink
HEIGHT: 3–5 feet
WIDTH: 3 feet
LIGHT: Partial–full shade
HARDINESS: Zones 5–9
FLOWERING SEASON: June–Oct.

This long-blooming plant tolerates heat and drought. Cutting it back in the early spring produces a fuller plant but may delay bloom time. It reseeds nicely but not invasively.

Geranium

CULTIVAR: 'Johnson's Blue'
COMMON NAME: Cranesbill
COLOR: Blue
HEIGHT: 18 inches
WIDTH: 18 inches
LIGHT: Partial shade–full sun
HARDINESS: Zones 5–8
FLOWERING SEASON: June–July

This easy-care plant may be invasive if the soil is too rich. Cut it back after it blooms.

Geranium sanguineum

COMMON NAME: Bloody Cranesbill
COLOR: Pink, white, magenta
HEIGHT: 8 inches
WIDTH: 12 inches
LIGHT: Partial shade–full sun
HARDINESS: Zones 4–8
FLOWERING SEASON: May–Sept.

Cut back this easy-care plant after it blooms.

Helianthemum

COMMON NAME: Sun Rose
COLOR: Yellow, pink, white, orange
HEIGHT: 6 inches
WIDTH: 8 inches
LIGHT: Full sun
HARDINESS: Zones 5–9
FLOWERING SEASON: May–June

Sun rose tolerates drought and heat. It needs little care, but cut it back after blooming.

Helenium autumnale

COMMON NAME: Sneezewort
COLOR: Yellow, orange, red
HEIGHT: Up to 4 feet
WIDTH: 24 inches
LIGHT: Full sun
HARDINESS: Zones 5–8
FLOWERING SEASON: Aug.–Sept.

This plant produces a clump-forming flower and offers good late-blooming color. It needs no deadheading.

Helleborus orientalis

COMMON NAME: Lenten Rose
COLOR: White, cream, rose
HEIGHT: 15–18 inches
WIDTH: 15 inches
LIGHT: Partial–full shade
HARDINESS: Zones 4–9
FLOWERING SEASON: March–May

This perennial will tolerate dry conditions in the summer. It is a long-living, easy-care plant that does not need to be divided. It reseeds nicely.

Hemerocallis

CULTIVAR: 'Hybrids Mix'
COMMON NAME: Daylily
COLOR: Variety
HEIGHT: 12–26 inches
WIDTH: 2 feet
LIGHT: Partial shade–full sun
HARDINESS: Zones 3–9
FLOWERING SEASON: June–Aug.

This tough, long-living plant tolerates hot, dry conditions. Divide it every four to five years. Repeat bloomers are 'Stella de Oro,' 'Bitsy,' 'Daily Bread,' and 'Fuzz Bunny.' Cut the stems back to the basal foliage after bloom.

Hesperis matronalis

CULTIVAR: 'Sweet Rocket Purple'
COMMON NAME: Dame's Rocket
COLOR: White, purple
HEIGHT: 2–3 feet
WIDTH: 2 feet
LIGHT: Partial shade–full sun
HARDINESS: Zones 4–9
FLOWERING SEASON: July–Aug.

Replace easy-care plant every two to three years as flowers diminish with age. Deadheading produces a second flush of flowers.

Heuchera micrantha

CULTIVAR: 'Bressingham Hybrids'
COMMON NAME: Coral Bells
COLOR: Pink, red
HEIGHT: 18 inches
WIDTH: 12 inches
LIGHT: Partial shade–full sun, especially in afternoon
HARDINESS: Zones 3–8
FLOWERING SEASON: May–Aug.

Deadhead this plant to prolong its bloom. Plant it in the spring so it can become established before winter, when it is susceptible to heaving.

Heuchera sanguinea

CULTIVAR: 'Splendens'
COMMON NAME: Coral Bells
COLOR: Scarlet red
HEIGHT: 28 inches
WIDTH: 12 inches
LIGHT: Partial shade–partial sun, especially in afternoon
HARDINESS: Zones 3–8
FLOWERING SEASON: May–Aug.

Deadhead this plant to prolong its bloom, and divide it in the spring every three years. Provide it with afternoon shade in hot, dry regions, and avoid drought.

Hibiscus moscheutos

COMMON NAME: Common Rose Mallow
COLOR: Rose, red, pink, white
HEIGHT: 4 feet
WIDTH: 5 feet
LIGHT: Full sun
HARDINESS: Zones 5–7
FLOWERING SEASON: July–frost

This plant's flowers, which can be ten inches across, last only one day. Deadhead it daily.

Hosta

COMMON NAME: Plantain Lily
COLOR: Lavender, white, mauve
HEIGHT: 6 inches–4 feet
WIDTH: 4 inches–6 feet
LIGHT: Partial–full shade
HARDINESS: Zones 3–9
FLOWERING SEASON: July–Sept.

Hostas come in a wide variety of leaf variations. They are grown for their leaf color, but some flowers are fragrant. Hostas with waxier leaves tolerate dry soils better than others. Slugs and snails are a real problem, but this is generally an easy-care plant.

Hypericum calycinum

COMMON NAME: Aaron's Beard, Rose of Sharon
COLOR: Yellow
HEIGHT: 24 inches
LIGHT: Partial shade–full sun
HARDINESS: Zones 5–9
FLOWERING SEASON: June–Sept.

This plant offers good ground cover. It spreads by runners but is easily controlled. Cut it down every other year to about six inches in the early spring. It needs no deadheading.

Iberis sempervirens

COMMON NAME: Candytuft
COLOR: White
HEIGHT: 12 inches
WIDTH: 16 inches
LIGHT: Full sun
HARDINESS: Zones 3–9
FLOWERING SEASON: May–June

You don't need to divide these plants because they have a subshrub growth habit. Stems may root when they come into contact with the soil, creating new plants. You can cut it back to a mound shape in the early spring.

Iris ensata, syn. I. kaempferi

COMMON NAME: Japanese Iris
COLOR: Blue, red, white, purple
HEIGHT: 3 feet
WIDTH: 24 inches
LIGHT: Partial shade–full sun
HARDINESS: Zones 4–9
FLOWERING SEASON: June–July

Divide this plant after it flowers and when its clump becomes too large.

Iris sibirica

COMMON NAME: Siberian Iris
COLOR: White, blue, purple
HEIGHT: 2–4 feet
WIDTH: 2 feet
LIGHT: Partial shade–full sun
HARDINESS: Zones 3–9
FLOWERING SEASON: May–June

This is a low-maintenance, multi-season plant that does not like to be divided. Remove the seed heads, which otherwise will reduce the vigor of next year's growth. For fresh growth, cut back all foliage after blooming.

Lamium maculatum

COMMON NAME: Spotted Deadnettle
COLOR: White, pink, mauve
HEIGHT: 8 inches
WIDTH: 3 feet
LIGHT: Shade–partial sun
HARDINESS: Zones 3–8
FLOWERING SEASON: May–June

The mottled-leaf foliage of this easy-care perennial offers good ground cover for dry, shady areas.

Lavandula angustifolia

COMMON NAME: Lavender
COLOR: Purple
HEIGHT: 12–24 inches
WIDTH: 24 inches
LIGHT: Full sun
HARDINESS: Zones 5–9
FLOWERING SEASON: June–Oct.

Lavender is an easy-care plant that tolerates drought conditions once it's established. For a second bloom in late summer or early fall, cut it back after it flowers. And every few years in the early spring, cut it back to six inches.

Leucanthemum x superbum

CULTIVAR: 'Little Silver Princess,' 'Snowcap'
COMMON NAME: Shasta Daisy
COLOR: White
HEIGHT: 12 inches
WIDTH: 12 inches
LIGHT: Full sun
HARDINESS: Zones 3–9
FLOWERING SEASON: June–July

Deadhead to prolong this plant's bloom time. The 'Snowcap' variety is long blooming.

Liatris

COMMON NAME: Gayfeather, Blazing Star
COLOR: Purple, white
HEIGHT: 2–3 feet
WIDTH: 2 feet
LIGHT: Full sun
HARDINESS: Zones 3–9
FLOWERING SEASON: July–Aug.

This easy-care plant tolerates drought. Deadhead it by cutting down the entire flower stalk, and you may get a second bloom. Plants need division every four to five years.

Ligularia dentata

COMMON NAME: Golden Groundsel
COLOR: Yellow orange
HEIGHT: 3–5 feet
WIDTH: 3 feet
LIGHT: Partial–full shade
HARDINESS: Zones 4–9
FLOWERING SEASON: July–Sept.

This plant's foliage has a tropical accent. Its leaves may wilt in the afternoon heat, but they revive in the evening. Slugs and snails can be a problem.

Lilium

COMMON NAME: Lily
COLOR: Variety
HEIGHT: 2–7 feet
WIDTH: 12 inches
LIGHT: Partial shade–full sun
HARDINESS: Zones 4–8
FLOWERING SEASON: July–Sept.

Lily is a good cut flower. After the bloom fades, cut off the stem's top third and leave the leaves to feed the bulb. Some oriental varieties of this easy-care plant are very fragrant.

Linum perenne

COMMON NAME: Perennial Flax
COLOR: Sky blue
HEIGHT: 12 inches
WIDTH: 12 inches
LIGHT: Full sun
HARDINESS: Zones 5–9
FLOWERING SEASON: June–Aug.

This is a light and airy plant with small, narrow leaves. After first bloom, shear it off by one-half for a repeat bloom. It is drought and heat tolerant.

Lobelia cardinalis

COMMON NAME: Cardinal Flower
COLOR: Red
HEIGHT: 36 inches
WIDTH: 12 inches
LIGHT: Partial shade–full sun
HARDINESS: Zones 2–9
FLOWERING SEASON: July–Sept.

The cardinal has narrow foliage and spiked flowers with a great red color. Deadhead it for longer bloom time.

Lupinus Russell Hybrids

COMMON NAME: Lupine
COLOR: Red, blue, yellow, pink, white
HEIGHT: 3–4 feet
WIDTH: 1½–2 feet
LIGHT: Partial–full shade
HARDINESS: Zones 4–7
FLOWERING SEASON: June–July

This short-lived perennial needs afternoon shade in hot areas. Cut it back after it flowers for possible rebloom.

Lysimachia clethroides

COMMON NAME: Gooseneck Loosestrife
COLOR: White
HEIGHT: 24 inches
WIDTH: 24 inches
LIGHT: Partial shade, sun
HARDINESS: Zones 4–9
FLOWERING SEASON: July–Aug.

This fragrant, fast-spreading perennial has saucer-shaped flowers on arching tips.

Meconopsis cambrica

COMMON NAME: Welsh Poppy
COLOR: Yellow
HEIGHT: 12 inches
WIDTH: 10 inches
LIGHT: Partial shade
HARDINESS: Zones 6–8
FLOWERING SEASON: May–Sept.

This perennial is easy to grow. It can reseed but not invasively. It likes woodland settings.

Mertensia pulmonarioides

COMMON NAME: Virginia Bluebells
COLOR: Bluish purple, blue, white
HEIGHT: 18–24 inches
WIDTH: 10 inches
LIGHT: Partial–full shade
HARDINESS: Zones 3–9
FLOWERING SEASON: May–June

This clump-forming plant with bell-shaped flowers is good for shady areas.

Monarda didyma

COMMON NAME: Bee Balm
COLOR: Violet pink, scarlet, white
HEIGHT: 2–4 feet
WIDTH: 4 feet
LIGHT: Partial shade–full sun
HARDINESS: Zones 4–8
FLOWERING SEASON: June–July

This long-blooming plant spreads by rhizomes. Divide it every two to three years to control its spread and keep plants strong. Deadhead it to prolong its bloom time. Watch for powdery mildew.

Myosotis sylvatica

COMMON NAME: Forget-me-not
COLOR: Blue, pink, white
HEIGHT: 8 inches
WIDTH: 2 feet
LIGHT: Partial shade
HARDINESS: Zones 3–8
FLOWERING SEASON: May–June

Plant this flower with spring bulbs. It reseeds each year and is grown as a biennial.

Nepeta x faassenii

COMMON NAME: Cat Mint
COLOR: Violet to lilac blue
HEIGHT: 3 feet
WIDTH: 3 feet
LIGHT: Partial shade–full sun
HARDINESS: Zones 3–8
FLOWERING SEASON: July–Sept.

For new growth of foliage, cut back this long-blooming plant after it flowers.

Oenothera missouriensis

COMMON NAME: Missouri Evening
   Primrose
COLOR: Yellow
HEIGHT: 10–12 inches
WIDTH: 20 inches
LIGHT: Partial shade–full sun
HARDINESS: Zones 5–8
FLOWERING SEASON: June–Aug.

This plant is drought tolerant and deer resistant. Its four-inch yellow flowers open in the afternoon and bloom throughout the summer months.

Oenothera speciosa

COMMON NAME: Pink Evening
   Primrose
COLOR: Pink
HEIGHT: 12 inches
WIDTH: 20 inches
LIGHT: Partial shade–full sun
HARDINESS: Zones 5–8
FLOWERING SEASON: June–Aug.

This drought- and heat-tolerant plant can become invasive.

Pachysandra terminalis

CULTIVAR: 'Silver Edge,' 'Green
   Sheen'
COMMON NAME: Japanese Spurge
COLOR: White
HEIGHT: 10 inches
WIDTH: 24 inches
LIGHT: Partial shade–full sun
HARDINESS: Zones 3–8
FLOWERING SEASON: April–May

This perennial, which needs acidic soil, offers good ground cover and stays green all winter. You can use its greenery in Christmas decorations.

Paeonia lactiflora

COMMON NAME: Common Garden
   Peony
COLOR: Pink, red, white
HEIGHT: 3 inches
WIDTH: 3 feet
LIGHT: Partial shade–full sun
HARDINESS: Zones 2–8
FLOWERING SEASON: May–June

Do not plant the eye of this perennial deeper than two inches below soil surface. Cut off spent blooms after it flowers.

Papaver orientale

COMMON NAME: Oriental Poppy
COLOR: Salmon, pink, red, orange,
   white
HEIGHT: 3–4 feet
WIDTH: 2 feet
LIGHT: Partial shade–full sun
HARDINESS: Zones 3–7
FLOWERING SEASON: May–June

This long-lived, easy-care plant will go dormant after blooming. It needs no deadheading. Combine planting with a later-blooming perennial for continuous color. Mulch first-year plants, and don't divide for at least six years.

Penstemon barbatus

CULTIVAR: 'Elfin Pink'
COMMON NAME: Beardlip Penstemon
COLOR: Pink, scarlet
HEIGHT: 2–3 feet
WIDTH: 1½ feet
LIGHT: Full sun
HARDINESS: Zones 3–9
FLOWERING SEASON: June–July

Treat this drought- and heat-tolerant plant as a biennial.

Penstemon comes in many colorful varieties.

Penstemon eatonii

COMMON NAME: Firecracker
    Penstemon
COLOR: Scarlet
HEIGHT: 18–30 inches
WIDTH: 8–14 inches
LIGHT: Partial shade–full sun
HARDINESS: Zone 3
FLOWERING SEASON: Spring

This is a hardy Intermountain area plant. It attracts hummingbirds and butterflies.

Penstemon palmeri

COMMON NAME: Scented Penstemon
COLOR: Bright pink
HEIGHT: 3–4 feet
WIDTH: 8–10 inches
LIGHT: Partial shade–full sun
HARDINESS: Zone 3
FLOWERING SEASON: June–Aug.

This flower is native to the Intermountain area. It attracts hummingbirds and butterflies and makes a great cut flower.

Penstemon strictus

COMMON NAME: Rocky Mountain
    Penstemon
COLOR: Blue
HEIGHT: 3 feet
WIDTH: 24 inches
LIGHT: Partial shade–full sun
HARDINESS: Zone 3
FLOWERING SEASON: Late spring

This penstemon tolerates drought, and it attracts hummingbirds and butterflies.

Penstemon whippleanus

COMMON NAME: Whipple's
    Penstemon
COLOR: Lavender–black purple
HEIGHT: 20–28 inches
WIDTH: 12 inches
LIGHT: Partial shade–full sun
HARDINESS: Zone 3
FLOWERING SEASON: July–Sept.

This flower is native to the Intermountain area.

Perovskia atriplicifolia

COMMON NAME: Russian Sage
COLOR: Lavender, blue
HEIGHT: 3–4 feet
WIDTH: 3–4 feet
LIGHT: Full sun
HARDINESS: Zones 5–9
FLOWERING SEASON: July–Aug.

This easy-care plant has good background flowers and needs no deadheading. It tolerates hot, dry conditions and should be cut back to within several inches of the ground in the early spring.

Phlox paniculata

COMMON NAME: Garden Phlox
COLOR: Pink, red, blue, white, purple
HEIGHT: 2–4 feet
WIDTH: 2 feet
LIGHT: Partial shade–full sun
HARDINESS: Zones 4–9
FLOWERING SEASON: July–Sept.

This long-blooming heavy feeder may require staking. Cut it back by half in the spring for later bloom, and divide it every three years. It is prone to mildew, but many new varieties are mildew resistant.

Physostegia virginiana

COMMON NAME: Obedient Plant
COLOR: Purple, white, lilac pink
HEIGHT: 3 feet
WIDTH: 24 inches
LIGHT: Partial shade–full sun
HARDINESS: Zones 2–9
FLOWERING SEASON: July–Sept.

This plant can spread vigorously, but it prefers moist soil.

Platycodon grandiflorus

COMMON NAME: Balloon Flower
COLOR: Blue, pink, white
HEIGHT: 2–3 feet
WIDTH: 2 feet
LIGHT: Full sun
HARDINESS: Zones 3–8
FLOWERING SEASON: July–Sept.

This plant is slow to become established, but it lives long and requires little maintenance. It is difficult to transplant and does not need to be divided for at least twenty years. 'Mariesii' is a shorter variety that does not need staking.

Polemonium caeruleum

COMMON NAME: Jacob's Ladder
COLOR: Blue, white
HEIGHT: 18–24 inches
WIDTH: 18 inches
LIGHT: Partial shade
HARDINESS: Zones 3–9
FLOWERING SEASON: June

These plants seldom need to be divided. Cut them back to basal foliage to promote a second bloom.

Polygonatum biflorum

COMMON NAME: Solomon's Seal
COLOR: White
HEIGHT: 2–3 feet
WIDTH: 24 inches
LIGHT: Partial shade–full sun
HARDINESS: Zones 4–8
FLOWERING SEASON: May–June

This taller accent plant has beautiful arching stems. It likes the shadiest part of the garden. Divide it by digging rhizomes.

Primula auricula

COMMON NAME: Primrose
COLOR: Variety
HEIGHT: 8 inches
WIDTH: 6 inches
LIGHT: Partial shade
HARDINESS: Zones 5–7
FLOWERING SEASON: April–May

Primrose is a great companion plant for tulips. Deadhead this easy-care plant regularly to prolong blooms.

Pulmonaria officinalis

CULTIVAR: 'Sissinghurst White'
COMMON NAME: Lungwort
COLOR: White
HEIGHT: 10–12 inches
WIDTH: 18 inches
LIGHT: Partial shade–full sun
HARDINESS: Zones 3–9
FLOWERING SEASON: April–May

This perennial offers good ground cover for shady areas. It is an easy-care plant, but it can get powdery mildew. To eliminate mildew, cut it back completely to develop new growth.

Pulsatilla vulgaris

COMMON NAME: Pasque Flower
COLOR: Purple, white
HEIGHT: 12 inches
WIDTH: 12 inches
LIGHT: Partial shade–full sun, especially in afternoon
HARDINESS: Zones 5–7
FLOWERING SEASON: April–June

This plant has attractive seed heads. Deadhead it regularly to extend bloom time. It does not require division for a long time, and it resents root disturbance.

Rudbeckia fulgida

COMMON NAME: Black-eyed Susan
COLOR: Golden yellow
HEIGHT: 18–30 inches
WIDTH: 24–30 inches
LIGHT: Partial shade–full sun
HARDINESS: Zones 3–9
FLOWERING SEASON: July–Sept.

This easy-care plant is drought and heat tolerant. Regular deadheading makes for a long bloom time. Its seed heads are food for birds, and its rhizome growth can create large colonies. Divide it every four years to it keep strong.

Rudbeckia hirta

CULTIVAR: 'Irish Eyes'
COMMON NAME: Black-eyed Susan
COLOR: Bright yellow
HEIGHT: 24–30 inches
WIDTH: 12 inches
LIGHT: Partial shade–full sun
HARDINESS: Zones 3–9
FLOWERING SEASON: July–Sept.

This is an easy-care, short-lived perennial that yields good cut flowers.

Salvia argentea

COMMON NAME: Silver Sage
COLOR: Gray
HEIGHT: 6 inches
WIDTH: 12 inches
LIGHT: Full sun
HARDINESS: Zones 4–7
FLOWERING SEASON: May–frost

This plant is grown for its fuzzy gray leaves. To keep it tidy, do not let it flower.

Salvia menorosa

COMMON NAME: Perennial Salvia
COLOR: Violet blue
HEIGHT: 18–36 inches
WIDTH: 24 inches
LIGHT: Full sun
HARDINESS: Zones 3–9
FLOWERING SEASON: June–Aug.

This tough, long-blooming, easy-care perennial is drought tolerant. Dividing should be done in the spring. Cut back spent flowers for a second bloom.

Sanguinaria canadensis

COMMON NAME: Bloodroot
COLOR: White
HEIGHT: 6 inches
WIDTH: 12 inches
LIGHT: Full shade
HARDINESS: Zones 3–9
FLOWERING SEASON: April–May

Bloodroot offers good ground cover for shady areas. 'Flore Pleno' has double flowers.

Saponaria ocymoides

COMMON NAME: Rock Soapwort
COLOR: Pink, white
HEIGHT: 4 inches
WIDTH: 18 inches
LIGHT: Partial shade–full sun
HARDINESS: Zones 3–8
FLOWERING SEASON: May–June

This is an easy-care, drought-resistant, mat-forming plant. Cut it back after it flowers.

Scabiosa columbaria

CULTIVAR: 'Butterfly Blue,' 'Pink Mist Feet'
COMMON NAME: Pincushion Flower
COLOR: Blue, pink
HEIGHT: 12 inches
WIDTH: 12 inches
LIGHT: Partial shade–full sun
HARDINESS: Zones 3–7
FLOWERING SEASON: May–Oct.

Deadheading prolongs the bloom on this easy-care plant and keeps it looking fresh. Divide it every three or four years if it becomes crowded. It can be prone to powdery mildew.

Sedum 'Herbstfreude'

CULTIVAR: 'Autumn Joy'
COMMON NAME: Sedum
COLOR: Pink, bronze, red
HEIGHT: 24 inches
WIDTH: 18 inches
LIGHT: Partial shade–full sun
HARDINESS: Zones 5–9
FLOWERING SEASON: Aug.–frost

Do not deadhead this low-maintenance, drought-tolerant, perennial until spring. This undemanding plant has outstanding winter interest.

Sedum kamtschaticum

COMMON NAME: Stonecrop
COLOR: Yellow
HEIGHT: 4 inches
WIDTH: 10 inches
LIGHT: Full sun
HARDINESS: Zones 5–9
FLOWERING SEASON: June–Sept.

Stonecrop tolerates drought and heat, and it yields good ground cover.

Sempervivum tectorum

COMMON NAME: Hen and chicks
COLOR: Pink, blue-green leaves
HEIGHT: 6 inches
WIDTH: 20 inches
LIGHT: Full sun
HARDINESS: Zones 3–9
FLOWERING SEASON: June–Aug.

Rust and crown rot can be a problem with this plant.

Sidalcea malviflora

CULTIVAR: 'Loveliness'
COMMON NAME: Checkerbloom, Mallow
COLOR: Pale pink
HEIGHT: 30 inches
WIDTH: 18 inches
LIGHT: Full sun
HARDINESS: Zones 5–9
FLOWERING SEASON: July–Sept.

This plant tolerates hot, dry conditions. Deadheading or cutting it back will promote a longer bloom time.

Solidago hybrids

COMMON NAME: Goldenrod
COLOR: Yellow
HEIGHT: 4–6 feet
WIDTH: 2 feet
LIGHT: Full sun
HARDINESS: Zones 3–9
FLOWERING SEASON: June–Sept.

Goldenrod is a drought-tolerant, easy-care plant. Cut it back by one-half in early June for more compact growth and to delay flowering by about a month.

Solidaster luteus

CULTIVAR: 'Lemore'
COMMON NAME: Solidaster
COLOR: Pale yellow
HEIGHT: 18 inches
WIDTH: 12 inches
LIGHT: Full sun
HARDINESS: Zones 5–8
FLOWERING SEASON: Aug.–Sept.

This plant is a cross of Solidago and Aster ptarmicoides, with daisy flower heads.

Stachys byzantina

COMMON NAME: Lambs' Ears
COLOR: Pink
HEIGHT: 12 inches
WIDTH: 18 inches
LIGHT: Full sun
HARDINESS: Zones 5–8
FLOWERING SEASON: June–July

This perennial tolerates hot, dry areas. It needs little care except for occasional dividing. Lambs' ears is grown for its hairy gray-green foliage rather than for its insignificant flowers.

Thalictrum aquilegiifolium

COMMON NAME: Meadow Rue
COLOR: Lavender, white
HEIGHT: 4–8 feet
WIDTH: 12–18 inches
LIGHT: Partial shade–full sun
HARDINESS: Zones 5–8
FLOWERING SEASON: June–July

This plant's delicate flowers on tall, slender stems create a light, airy effect. It can reseed.

Thalictrum rochebruneanum

CULTIVAR: 'Lavender Mist'
COMMON NAME: Meadow Rue
COLOR: Lavender
HEIGHT: 5 feet
WIDTH: 12 inches
LIGHT: Partial shade–partial sun
HARDINESS: Zones 5–8
FLOWERING SEASON: July–Aug.

This plant is like *aquilegiifolium*, but it blooms later in the season.

Thermopsis caroliniana, syn. T. villosa

COMMON NAME: Carolina Lupine
COLOR: Yellow
HEIGHT: 3–5 feet
WIDTH: 24 inches
LIGHT: Partial shade–full sun
HARDINESS: Zones 3–9
FLOWERING SEASON: May–June

This perennial can tolerate drought conditions. Its flowers attract bees, and it needs no deadheading. This can be an invasive weed in southern Utah.

Thymus

COMMON NAME: Thyme
COLOR: Lavender, rose, white
HEIGHT: 3–12 inches
WIDTH: 12–18 inches
LIGHT: Full sun
HARDINESS: Zones 5–9
FLOWERING SEASON: June–July

Thyme comes in many different varieties. It offers good ground cover and tolerates hot, dry conditions.

Tiarella wherryi

COMMON NAME: Foam Flower
COLOR: White, pinkish white
HEIGHT: 4–12 inches
WIDTH: 12 inches
LIGHT: Partial shade–full sun
HARDINESS: Zones 3–8
FLOWERING SEASON: May–July

This plant has star-shaped, fluffy flowers and can be grown as a ground cover. Deadheading makes it look tidy and prolongs bloom time.

Trollius europaeus

COMMON NAME: Globeflower
COLOR: Shades of yellow
HEIGHT: 36 inches
WIDTH: 24 inches
LIGHT: Partial shade–full sun
HARDINESS: Zones 3–9
FLOWERING SEASON: June–July

This easy-care plant produces good cut flowers. Cut stems back after blooming.

Verbascum

COMMON NAME: Mullein
COLOR: Purple, yellow, rose, white
HEIGHT: 3–6 feet
WIDTH: 1½–2 feet
LIGHT: Partial shade–full sun
HARDINESS: Zones 4–8
FLOWERING SEASON: June–Sept.

This is a short-lived, easy-care, self-seeding perennial or biennial. Deadheading can prolong bloom time through Sept.

Veronica austriaca

CULTIVAR: 'Crater Lake Blue'
COMMON NAME: Hungarian Speedwell
COLOR: Deep blue
HEIGHT: 18 inches
WIDTH: 24 inches
LIGHT: Full sun
HARDINESS: Zones 3–9
FLOWERING SEASON: June–July

Cut back this plant by half after it flowers. It is prone to powdery mildew.

Veronica spicata

COMMON NAME: Spike Speedwell
COLOR: Pink, blue, white
HEIGHT: 12–18 inches
WIDTH: 24 inches
LIGHT: Full sun
HARDINESS: Zones 3–9
FLOWERING SEASON: June–Aug.

This perennial's plume-like arching flowers are good in floral arrangements. Deadhead to prolong bloom time. It may need staking, and it should be divided every two-three years.

Vinca major

COMMON NAME: Greater Periwinkle
COLOR: Blue
HEIGHT: 8 inches
WIDTH: 36 inches
LIGHT: Partial shade–full sun
HARDINESS: Zones 4–9
FLOWERING SEASON: May–Sept.

This plant can be invasive, but it is deer resistant and offers good ground cover in controlled areas.

Vinca minor

COMMON NAME: Creeping Myrtle, Dwarf Periwinkle
COLOR: Blue, white
HEIGHT: 8 inches
WIDTH: 36 inches
LIGHT: Partial shade
HARDINESS: Zones 4–7
FLOWERING SEASON: May–Sept.

This perennial is a tidier, less-invasive, dwarf form of Vinca major. It offers good ground cover for shady areas.

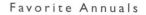

Favorite

Annuals

Agapanthus

COMMON NAME: Lily-of-the-Nile
COLOR: Blue
HEIGHT: 24–36 inches
WIDTH: 12–18 inches
LIGHT: Partial–full sun
FLOWERING SEASON: July–Sept.

This annual produces flowers on tall stems with long, flat foliage. It needs liquid fertilizer in the spring and throughout bloom time. It is drought and heat tolerant.

Ageratum houstonianum

COMMON NAME: Floss Flower
COLOR: Blue, pink, white
HEIGHT: 6–18 inches
WIDTH: 8–12 inches
LIGHT: Full sun
FLOWERING SEASON: June until frost

Deadhead this plant regularly to keep it blooming. It needs extra water in hot, dry weather, and it does not like windy, exposed sites.

Amaranthus tricolor

CULTIVAR: 'Joseph's Coat'
COMMON NAME: Chinese Spinach
COLOR: Crimson and other colors
HEIGHT: 2–3 feet
WIDTH: 12–18 inches
LIGHT: Partial–full sun
FLOWERING SEASON: July–Oct.

This annual's blossoms, which grow up to eighteen inches wide, can be used in flower arrangements. Water it well during dry spells.

Antirrhinum majus

COMMON NAME: Snapdragon
COLOR: Variety
HEIGHT: 6–48 inches
WIDTH: 6–24 inches
LIGHT: Full sun
FLOWERING SEASON: July–Oct.

This annual will sometimes over-winter in protected areas, and it can reseed. When the plant is about three inches tall, pinch off its top half to encourage bushy growth. Deadhead throughout the summer. Favorite varieties are 'Butterfly Mix,' 'Floral Showers,' 'Rocket Mix,' and 'Sonnet Series.'

Asarina procumbens

COMMON NAME: Climbing
    Snapdragon
COLOR: Yellow
HEIGHT: 2 inches
WIDTH: 24 inches
LIGHT: Partial shade–full sun
FLOWERING SEASON: July–Sept.

The plant is a climbing or hanging vine with long, trumpet-shaped blos-soms that cascade down.

Begonia semperflorens

COMMON NAME: Fibrous Begonia
COLOR: Variety
HEIGHT: 6–12 inches
WIDTH: 5–15 inches
LIGHT: Partial shade–partial sun
FLOWERING SEASON: June–Sept.

Do not plant this begonia outdoors until June because it is frost sensi-tive. It combines nicely with the tuberous variety of begonia.

Begonia tuberhybrida

COMMON NAME: Tuberous Begonia
COLOR: Variety
HEIGHT: 12 inches
WIDTH: 6–12 inches
LIGHT: Full shade
FLOWERING SEASON: June–Sept.

This plant produces vibrant double and semidouble flowers. Plant in shade with the pointed tip of the leaves toward the sun.

Brachyscome iberidifolia

COMMON NAME: Swan River Daisy
COLOR: Purple and pink shades
HEIGHT: 12–18 inches
WIDTH: 12–18 inches
LIGHT: Partial shade–sun
FLOWERING SEASON: June–Aug.

This plant tolerates heat well but needs plenty of water. About once a month, cut off dead flower heads to prevent seed formation.

Brassica oleracea

COMMON NAME: Ornamental
    Cabbage or Kale
COLOR: Pink, purple, green foliage
HEIGHT: 12–18 inches
WIDTH: 12–18 inches
LIGHT: Full sun
FLOWERING SEASON: June–late fall

This annual's edible leaves are bril-liant pink and purple, especially in cool fall weather with light frost. It is grown for its foliage rather than its blossoms. Remove blossom stems as they appear.

Browallia speciosa

COMMON NAME: Bush Violet
COLOR: Soft blue and white
HEIGHT: 12–16 inches
WIDTH: 12–16 inches
LIGHT: Partial shade–partial sun
FLOWERING SEASON: May–Aug.

Pinch back the stems of this annual by one-half in early June to promote spreading and to prevent leggy growth.

Calendula officinalis

COMMON NAME: Pot Marigold or English Marigold
COLOR: Variety
HEIGHT: 1–2 feet
WIDTH: 12–18 inches
LIGHT: Partial shade–full sun
FLOWERING SEASON: June–Oct.

Plant this annual's seeds in early spring, and you'll enjoy ten weeks of bloom in the summer. Pinch off new growth to encourage bushiness. Deadhead regularly to prolong bloom season. This plant is drought and heat tolerant.

Calibracoa

COMMON NAME: Million Bells
COLOR: Variety
HEIGHT: 12 inches
WIDTH: 12 inches
LIGHT: Full sun
FLOWERING SEASON: June–Sept.

This annual makes a great container plant and is available in trailing and upright varieties. It needs nitrogen fertilizer every month during the bloom season.

Callistephus chinensis

COMMON NAME: China Aster
COLOR: White, pink, blue
HEIGHT: 9–18 inches
WIDTH: 9–18 inches
LIGHT: Full sun–partial shade
FLOWERING SEASON: Aug.–Sept.

This annual produces good color in late summer and autumn. Deadhead it regularly, and plant it in a different location each year to ward off disease.

Campanula medium

COMMON NAME: Canterbury Bells
COLOR: Pink, white, blue
HEIGHT: 18–30 inches
WIDTH: 12 inches
LIGHT: Partial shade–full sun
FLOWERING SEASON: May–June

This perennial grows well as an annual on Temple Square. Blooms may be single, semidouble, or double. Protect it from slugs and snails, and remove faded blossoms to prolong bloom time. It can be a high-maintenance plant.

Catharanthus roseus

COMMON NAME: Vinca
COLOR: White, pink, red
HEIGHT: 6–12 inches
WIDTH: 6–12 inches
LIGHT: Full sun–partial shade
FLOWERING SEASON: June–Oct.

This annual is good for borders. It tolerates drought and hot sun.

Celosia argentea
CULTIVAR: 'Plumosa Group'
COMMON NAME: Cockscomb
COLOR: Pink and white
HEIGHT: 12–16 inches
WIDTH: 12–16 inches
LIGHT: Full sun
FLOWERING SEASON: June–Oct.

This plant produces flowers with a feathery, pyramid shape.

Chrysanthemum paludosum (Leucanthemum paludosum)
COMMON NAME: Paludosum Daisy
COLOR: White
HEIGHT: 12 inches
WIDTH: 12 inches
LIGHT: Full sun–partial shade
FLOWERING SEASON: May–Oct.

This wonderful white summer flower can reseed. Share it or transplant it to other areas in your garden.

Cleome hassleriana
COMMON NAME: Spider Flower
COLOR: White, purple, and pink
HEIGHT: 5 feet
WIDTH: 18 inches
LIGHT: Full sun–partial shade
FLOWERING SEASON: June–Oct.

This plant's prominent flower heads on sturdy stems grow taller as the summer progresses. It does best if planted by seed each year.

Coleus (Solenostemon)
CULTIVAR: 'Wizard Series'
COMMON NAME: Coleus, Painted Nettle
COLOR: Pinks, reds, purples, rusts
HEIGHT: 8–20 inches
WIDTH: 15 inches
LIGHT: Partial–full shade
FLOWERING SEASON: June–first frost

This plant, grown for its colorful leaves, is a good plant for shady areas. Pinch off young shoots to encourage bushiness, and remove flower stems as they appear.

Cosmos
CULTIVAR: 'Lemon Twist,' 'Sonata Dwarf Mix'
COMMON NAME: Cosmos
COLOR: Yellow, pink, purple, white, orange, scarlet
HEIGHT: 12–36 inches
WIDTH: 8–12 inches
LIGHT: Full sun
FLOWERING SEASON: June–first frost

This annual is easy to grow from seed and makes a good cut flower. It can reseed.

Dahlia
COMMON NAME: Annual Dahlia
COLOR: Variety
HEIGHT: 10–18 inches
WIDTH: 8–10 inches
LIGHT: Full sun
FLOWERING SEASON: June–first frost

This annual, grown from seed, is a smaller version of tuberous dahlias. Keep it deadheaded.

Ipomoea tricolor

CULTIVAR: 'Heavenly Blue'
COMMON NAME: Morning Glory
COLOR: Blue
HEIGHT: 8–10 feet
LIGHT: Full sun
FLOWERING SEASON: July–Oct.

This plant is a fast-growing vine, and it produces flowers that bloom from dawn until mid-afternoon and last only one day each. It is best grown from seeds that have been soaked overnight before planting. Sow seeds directly in the garden, and do not disturb plant roots.

Lantana camara

COMMON NAME: Lantana, Shrub Verbena
COLOR: Yellow, orange, pink
HEIGHT: 12–18 inches
WIDTH: 18–24 inches
LIGHT: Full sun
FLOWERING SEASON: June–Oct.

This annual tolerates hot, dry conditions. The trailing variety is nice for baskets and containers.

Lobelia erinus

COMMON NAME: Lobelia
COLOR: Purple, lavender, blue, white, crimson, rose
HEIGHT: 4–8 inches
WIDTH: 6–8 inches
LIGHT: Partial shade
FLOWERING SEASON: May–Oct.

This is a good edging plant. It needs half a day of shade and does not like direct hot sun. Fertilize it every two weeks in the spring and early summer with a balanced liquid fertilizer. From July to September, use a nitrogen-free fertilizer.

Lobularia maritima

COMMON NAME: Sweet Alyssum
COLOR: White, pink, purple
HEIGHT: 3–6 inches
WIDTH: 8–12 inches
LIGHT: Full sun
FLOWERING SEASON: June–frost

This annual is a good edging and container plant. If left in the garden, it will reseed to a white variety the following year. Sweet alyssum will need to be thinned. Favorites are 'Easter Bonnet,' 'Oriental Night,' and 'Wonderland Mix.'

Lunaria annua

COMMON NAME: Honesty Plant, Money Plant, or Silver Dollars
COLOR: Purple, white
HEIGHT: 36 inches
WIDTH: 12 inches
LIGHT: Partial–full sun
FLOWERING SEASON: May–June

Let this annual go to seed, and artistically remove those that will not fit into your design. It makes a good cut flower.

Mandevilla laxa

COMMON NAME: Chilean Jasmine
COLOR: Pink
HEIGHT: 8–10 feet
LIGHT: Partial–full sun
FLOWERING SEASON: June–Oct.

This plant likes a humid environment. Use it in a protected area.

Moluccella laevis

COMMON NAME: Bells of Ireland
COLOR: Green
HEIGHT: 24–36 inches
WIDTH: 6–8 inches
LIGHT: Full sun–partial shade
FLOWERING SEASON: June–Oct.

This annual produces a good cut flower, especially for dried floral arrangements. Its green blossoms turn pale beige after drying.

Nephrolepis exaltata

CULTIVAR: 'Bostoniensis'
COMMON NAME: Boston Fern
COLOR: Green
HEIGHT: 3 feet
WIDTH: 6 feet
LIGHT: Full shade–partial sun
FLOWERING SEASON: May–Oct.

Traditionally a houseplant, this fern may be used as an annual in the shade garden and moved indoors for winter. Its green foliage makes it a good accent plant.

Nicotiana alata

CULTIVAR: 'Nicki Series'
COMMON NAME: Flowering Tobacco
COLOR: Pink, red, rose, white
HEIGHT: 16–18 inches
WIDTH: 12 inches
LIGHT: Partial shade–sun
FLOWERING SEASON: June–frost

This dwarf form is strongly fragrant in the evening.

Nicotiana x sanderae

CULTIVAR: 'Domino Series'
COMMON NAME: Flowering Tobacco
COLOR: Red, salmon pink, white, lime
HEIGHT: 12–18 inches
WIDTH: 12–16 inches
LIGHT: Partial shade–sun
FLOWERING SEASON: June–frost

Occasional deadheading can improve the appearance of this annual.

Nicotiana sylvestris

COLOR: White
HEIGHT: Up to 5 feet
WIDTH: 24 inches
LIGHT: Partial shade–sun
FLOWERING SEASON: Late June–frost

This annual produces sweet-scented, long-tubed, trumpet-shaped flowers.

Nierembergia caerulea

COMMON NAME: Cup Flower
COLOR: Purple, white
HEIGHT: 8 inches
WIDTH: 8 inches
LIGHT: Partial–full sun
FLOWERING SEASON: June–Oct.

This annual likes shade in hot weather. Favorite varieties are 'Mont Blanc' and 'Purple Robe.'

Nigella damascena

COMMON NAME: Love-in-a-mist
COLOR: White, blue
HEIGHT: 18–24 inches
WIDTH: 6–12 inches
LIGHT: Full sun
FLOWERING SEASON: June–Oct.

This plant dries out quickly in hot weather. If you grow it from seed, sow seeds directly in the garden. It reseeds and self-sows readily but needs to be artistically thinned each spring.

Nolana humifusa

CULTIVAR: 'Little Bells'
COMMON NAME: Nolana
COLOR: Lilac blue
HEIGHT: 6 inches
WIDTH: 18 inches
LIGHT: Partial–full sun
FLOWERING SEASON: May–Sept.

This spreading plant is good for edging and the front of borders.

Ocimum basilicum

CULTIVAR: 'Purple Ruffles'
COMMON NAME: Basil, Sweet Basil
COLOR: Purple foliage
HEIGHT: 12–20 inches
WIDTH: 6–12 inches
LIGHT: Full sun
FLOWERING SEASON: June–first frost

This plant produces aromatic, edible foliage. Remove its flowers to encourage leaf growth. It can reseed.

Osteospermum hybrids

COMMON NAME: African Daisy
COLOR: White, pink, yellow, purple
HEIGHT: 12 inches
WIDTH: 6–8 inches
LIGHT: Full sun
FLOWERING SEASON: May–Oct.

Deadhead this annual regularly to prolong bloom time.

Papaver nudicaule

COMMON NAME: Iceland Poppy
COLOR: Pink, white, yellow, orange
HEIGHT: 1–1½ feet
WIDTH: 4–6 inches
LIGHT: Full sun
FLOWERING SEASON: May–July

Sometimes grown as a biennial or tender perennial, Iceland poppy seeds are best sown in the fall. Keep it deadheaded to prolong bloom time.

Pelargonium

COMMON NAME: Zonal Geranium
COLOR: White, pink, salmon, red
HEIGHT: 12–24 inches
WIDTH: 12–24 inches
LIGHT: Full sun
FLOWERING SEASON: May–Oct.

Geranium likes some afternoon shade in hot weather. Deadhead it throughout the summer to keep it blooming. Ivy geraniums (P. peltatum) have a trailing habit and are good for hanging baskets and containers.

Pennisetum setaceum

COMMON NAME: Fountain Grass
COLOR: Reddish purple foxtails
HEIGHT: 18–30 inches
WIDTH: 12–24 inches
LIGHT: Full sun
FLOWERING SEASON: July–Sept.

This plant's burgundy-bronze leaves bleach to a straw color in the winter. Leave it in the garden for winter interest.

Penstemon gloxiniodes

COMMON NAME: Beard Tongue
COLOR: Variety
HEIGHT: 2–3 feet
WIDTH: 2 feet
LIGHT: Full sun
FLOWERING SEASON: June–Oct.

This perennial is often used as an annual on Temple Square. Deadheading increases its number of blooms and the likelihood of perennial behavior. Once it becomes established, it is heat and drought tolerant.

Petunia x hybrida

COMMON NAME: Petunia
COLOR: Variety
HEIGHT: 12–24 inches
WIDTH: 24–36 inches
LIGHT: Full sun
FLOWERING SEASON: May–Oct.

To prolong blooming, pinch back this plant by up to one-half when it becomes long and leggy, usually in mid-July. The 'Cascade' series has a trailing habit good for hanging baskets and containers. The 'Fantasy' series has smaller, dense blooms and does not need to be deadheaded.

Sargent crabapple trees overlook a colorful cornucopia of marigolds, salvias, impatiens, cleomes, ageratums, coleus, and vincas.

Phlox drummondii

COMMON NAME: Annual Phlox
COLOR: Variety
HEIGHT: 4–18 inches
WIDTH: 10 inches
LIGHT: Full sun
FLOWERING SEASON: May–Aug.

The plant blooms throughout the summer if it is deadheaded regularly.

Portulaca grandiflora

COMMON NAME: Moss Rose
COLOR: Variety
HEIGHT: 4–8 inches
WIDTH: 12 inches
LIGHT: Full sun
FLOWERING SEASON: June–Oct.

This is a good plant for hot, dry areas. It can reseed for next year. 'Sundial Series' is a favorite.

Salvia coccinea

CULTIVAR: 'Coral Nymph,' 'Lady in Red'
COMMON NAME: Texas Sage
COLOR: Coral red
HEIGHT: 18–24 inches
WIDTH: 6–12 inches
LIGHT: Full sun–partial shade
FLOWERING SEASON: June–Oct.

Keep this annual deadheaded for continuous bright, airy spikes of blooms.

Salvia farinacea

CULTIVAR: 'Victoria Blue,' 'Silver White'
COMMON NAME: Salvia
COLOR: Blue, white
HEIGHT: 18–24 inches
WIDTH: 6–12 inches
LIGHT: Full–partial sun
FLOWERING SEASON: June–Oct.

Keep this plant deadheaded for continuous blooms.

Sanvitalia procumbens

CULTIVAR: 'Mandarin Orange'
COMMON NAME: Creeping Zinnia
COLOR: Orange
HEIGHT: 4–8 inches
WIDTH: Trailing to 12 inches long
LIGHT: Full sun
FLOWERING SEASON: June–Oct.

This heat-tolerant annual produces a trailing habit that works well in hanging baskets and containers.

Scaevola aemula

CULTIVAR: 'Blue Wonder'
COMMON NAME: Fairy Fan Flower
COLOR: Purple blue
HEIGHT: 6 inches
WIDTH: Trailing to 5 feet long
LIGHT: Partial–full sun
FLOWERING SEASON: June–Oct.

This is a great spreading plant that works well in borders. It's also a good container plant. Prune it to limit its growth.

Schizanthus x wisetonensis

COMMON NAME: Butterfly Flower
COLOR: Variety
HEIGHT: 18 inches
WIDTH: 9–12 inches
LIGHT: Partial sun–partial shade
FLOWERING SEASON: June–Aug.

This annual needs more shade in hot weather. Pinching it back makes it bushier.

Tagetes

COMMON NAME: African Marigold, American Marigold
COLOR: Yellow, gold, orange, white
HEIGHT: 6–36 inches
WIDTH: 6–24 inches
LIGHT: Full sun
FLOWERING SEASON: June–Oct.

Deadheading this annual increases its bloom. The white variety needs afternoon shade.

Tagetes patula

COMMON NAME: French Marigold
COLOR: Yellow, gold
HEIGHT: 6–12 inches
WIDTH: 6–12 inches
LIGHT: Full sun
FLOWERING SEASON: June–Oct.

The French marigold is a small, easy-to-grow plant.

Tagetes tenuifolia

CULTIVAR: 'Lemon Gem'
COMMON NAME: Signet Marigold, Gem Marigold
COLOR: Lemon yellow, orange
HEIGHT: 6–9 inches
WIDTH: 6–9 inches
LIGHT: Full sun
FLOWERING SEASON: June–Sept.

This annual produces delicate flowers with feathery foliage and edible petals. It can reseed for next year's bloom.

Thunbergia alata

CULTIVAR: 'Suzie Hybrids'
COMMON NAME: Black-eyed Susan Vine
COLOR: White, yellow, orange
HEIGHT: Trailing vine to 8 feet
LIGHT: Full sun
FLOWERING SEASON: mid-June–Oct.

This is a good annual for fences, trellises, hanging baskets, containers, and rock walls. It produces fragrant flowers.

Torenia fournieri

CULTIVAR: 'Clown Series,' 'Summer Wave Series'
COMMON NAME: Wishbone Flower
COLOR: Blue, pink, purple, white
HEIGHT: 8–10 inches
WIDTH: 6–9 inches
LIGHT: Partial shade–partial sun
FLOWERING SEASON: June–Oct.

This is a great accent plant for border fronts. The 'Summer Wave' is the best variety for Utah.

Tropaeolum majus

COMMON NAME: Nasturtium
COLOR: Variety
HEIGHT: 6–18 inches
WIDTH: 6–18 inches
LIGHT: Full–partial sun
FLOWERING SEASON: June–Oct.

This annual is best grown from seed. Sow seeds outdoors after winter's last frost. Its leaves and flowers are edible.

Verbena canadensis

CULTIVAR: 'Homestead Purple'
COMMON NAME: Rose Vervain
COLOR: Purple
HEIGHT: 18 inches
WIDTH: 18–36 inches
LIGHT: Full sun
FLOWERING SEASON: June–Oct.

This speading plant is not winter hardy.

Verbena x hybrida

COMMON NAME: Verbena
COLOR: Variety
HEIGHT: 6–18 inches
WIDTH: 12–24
LIGHT: Full sun
FLOWERING SEASON: June–Oct.

Favorite varieties of this annual are Novalis Series, Romance Series, 'Imagination,' and 'Tapien.' 'Peaches and Cream' has a spreading habit good for ground cover, rock gardens, and container plantings.

Viola x wittrockiana

COMMON NAME: Pansy
COLOR: Variety
HEIGHT: 6–12 inches
WIDTH: 6–12 inches
LIGHT: Partial–full sun
FLOWERING SEASON: April–Oct.

Pansies do best when planted in the fall as a companion to spring bulbs. They like cool weather. Use mulch to protect the roots from the summer heat. For fall bloom, pinch back plants by one-half when the weather gets hot.

Zinnia haageana, syn. Z. angustifolia

COMMON NAME: Zinnia
COLOR: Rose pink, salmon pink, white, orange
HEIGHT: 8–12 inches
WIDTH: 12 inches
LIGHT: Full sun
FLOWERING SEASON: June–Oct.

This is a good easy-care plant for hot, dry gardens. Sow seeds in garden after winter's last frost. Deadhead regularly to keep plants blooming. Look for mildew-resistant varieties.

Favorite

Bulbs

Allium shubertii

COMMON NAME: Onion

COLOR: Pale purple flowers

HEIGHT: 12–16 inches

FLOWERING SEASON: Late spring to early summer

This bulb produces excellent cut and dried flowers. It is long blooming, with blooms that explode like fireworks. Its basal leaves die back before flowering, and it is sensitive to frost.

Anemone blanda

CULTIVAR: 'Alba'

COMMON NAME: Grecian Windflower

COLOR: White

HEIGHT: 4 inches

FLOWERING SEASON: Early spring

This long-blooming bulb likes light, sandy soil. It produces dainty daisy-shaped flowers and is excellent for naturalizing.

Anemone blanda

CULTIVAR: 'Blue Star'

COMMON NAME: Grecian Windflower

COLOR: Blue

HEIGHT: 4 inches

FLOWERING SEASON: Early

This long-blooming bulb likes light sandy soil. It produces dainty daisy-shaped flowers and is excellent for naturalizing.

Chionodoxa

CULTIVAR: 'Sardensis'
COMMON NAME: Glory of the Snow
COLOR: Blue
HEIGHT: 4 inches
FLOWERING SEASON: Early

Glory of the snow produces star-shaped flowers that sometimes appear even before the snow has melted. It is excellent for naturalizing.

Eremurus

CULTIVAR: 'Isabellinus cultivars'
COMMON NAME: Foxtail Lily, Desert Candle
COLOR: Orange, yellow, pink
HEIGHT: 6 feet
FLOWERING SEASON: Early summer

This bulb performs best when planted in the fall. It produces tall spires of star-shaped flowers that last long when cut.

Erythronium

CULTIVAR: 'Grandiflorum'
COMMON NAME: Trout Lily, Dog's-tooth Violet
COLOR: Yellow flowers
HEIGHT: 12 inches
FLOWERING SEASON: Early

This bulb does well under deciduous trees and shrubs, or in rock gardens. It produces lily-like flowers and is excellent for naturalizing.

Fritillaria

CULTIVAR: 'Imperialis'
COMMON NAME: Crown Imperial
COLOR: Orange, yellow, red
HEIGHT: 1–3 feet
FLOWERING SEASON: Late

This tolerant species produces bell-shaped flowers that hang down. It likes moist soil and is good for naturalizing.

Hyacinthus orientalis

CULTIVAR: 'Delft Blue,' 'City of Haarlem,' 'Lady Derby,' 'L'Innocence'
COMMON NAME: Hyacinth
COLOR: Blue, yellow, pink, white
HEIGHT: 10 inches
FLOWERING SEASON: Early

Hyacinth produces fragrant flowers. Wear gloves when handling bulbs, which can irritate the skin. Plant in well-draining soil.

Narcissus

COMMON NAME: Daffodil
COLOR: Variety
HEIGHT: 14 inches
FLOWERING SEASON: Late

'Ambergate' produces large cup-shaped flowers that develop their color best in shade.

Narcissus

CULTIVAR: 'Baby Moon'
COMMON NAME: Daffodil
COLOR: Pale yellow
HEIGHT: 7 inches
FLOWERING SEASON: Late

'Baby Moon' produces fragrant flowers and grass-like foliage. It is good for rock gardens (Jonquilla).

Narcissus

CULTIVAR: 'Bell Song'
COMMON NAME: Daffodil
COLOR: Ivory cup, pink petal
HEIGHT: 14–16 inches
FLOWERING SEASON: Mid-season

'Bell Song' produces two to three flower stems with one or two fragrant flowers per stem (Jonquilla).

Narcissus

CULTIVAR: 'Cheerfulness'
COMMON NAME: Daffodil
COLOR: White
HEIGHT: 14 inches
FLOWERING SEASON: Late

'Cheerfulness' produces fragrant double flowers (Double).

Narcissus

CULTIVAR: 'Geranium'
COMMON NAME: Daffodil
COLOR: Orange cup, white petal
HEIGHT: 18 inches
FLOWERING SEASON: Late

'Geranium' is a multiflowering bulb that produces fragrant flowers (Tazetta).

Narcissus

CULTIVAR: 'Hawera'
COMMON NAME: Daffodil
COLOR: Lemon yellow
HEIGHT: 12 inches
FLOWERING SEASON: Early

'Hawera' produces multiple long-lasting flowers with a light fragrance. It is good for naturalizing (Triandrus).

Narcissus

CULTIVAR: 'Ice Wings'
COMMON NAME: Daffodil
COLOR: White
HEIGHT: 8 inches
FLOWERING SEASON: Early to mid-season

'Ice Wings' produces two to three light-fragrance flowers per stem. It is good for naturalizing (Triandrus).

Some of the different flower forms of narcissus

Trumpet and large-cupped

Small-cupped

Double

Poeticus

Triandrus and Jonquilla

Tazetta

Narcissus

CULTIVAR: 'Jack Snipe'
COMMON NAME: Daffodil
COLOR: Yellow cup, white petal
HEIGHT: 8 inches
FLOWERING SEASON: Early to mid-season

'Jack Snipe' produces long-lasting flowers. It is good for rock gardens (Cyclamineus).

Narcissus

CULTIVAR: 'Minnow'
COMMON NAME: Daffodil
COLOR: Cream cup, gold petal
HEIGHT: 6 inches
FLOWERING SEASON: Early

This dwarf is excellent for naturalizing. It produces four to five fragrant flowers per stem (Tazetta).

Narcissus

CULTIVAR: 'Mount Hood'
COMMON NAME: Daffodil
COLOR: White
HEIGHT: 18 inches
FLOWERING SEASON: Early

'Mount Hood' produces a long-lasting large flower (Trumpet).

Narcissus

CULTIVAR: 'Pipit'
COMMON NAME: Daffodil
COLOR: White cup, yellow petal
HEIGHT: 8 inches
FLOWERING SEASON: Mid-season

'Pipit' produces two to three fragrant flowers per stem that last three to four weeks (Jonquilla).

Narcissus

CULTIVAR: 'Romance'
COMMON NAME: Daffodil
COLOR: Pink cup, white petal
HEIGHT: 16 inches
FLOWERING SEASON: Mid-season

'Romance' is the best of the pink-cupped narcissi (Large cupped).

Narcissus

CULTIVAR: 'Spellbinder'
COMMON NAME: Daffodil
COLOR: Yellow cup, chartreuse petal
HEIGHT: 18 inches
FLOWERING SEASON: Early

'Spellbinder' produces one large, slightly scented, four-inch flower per stem (Trumpet).

Narcissus

CULTIVAR: 'Tahiti'
COMMON NAME: Daffodil
COLOR: Yellow crowned, orange
HEIGHT: 18 inches
FLOWERING SEASON: Mid-season

'Tahiti' has double blooms and yellow perianths with frilly orange-red centers (Double).

Narcissus

CULTIVAR: 'Tête-à-Tête'
COMMON NAME: Daffodil
COLOR: Yellow
HEIGHT: 8 inches
FLOWERING SEASON: Early

This dwarf blooms at the same time crocus blooms and is excellent for naturalizing (miscellaneous cultivar).

Narcissus

CULTIVAR: 'Thalia'
COMMON NAME: Daffodil
COLOR: White
HEIGHT: 10 inches
FLOWERING SEASON: Mid-season

'Thalia' produces good, long-lasting, fragrant flowers (Triandrus).

Narcissus

CULTIVAR: 'Unsurpassable'
COMMON NAME: Daffodil
COLOR: Yellow
HEIGHT: 18 inches
FLOWERING SEASON: Early

This bulb produces one of the largest flowers. It is excellent for naturalizing and good for indoor forcing (Trumpet).

Narcissus

CULTIVAR: 'White Lion'
COMMON NAME: Daffodil
COLOR: White crowned, yellow
HEIGHT: 18 inches
FLOWERING SEASON: Mid-season

This bulb produces double gardenia-like fragrant flowers. It is a good naturalizer (Double).

Narcissus, commonly known as daffodils, are separated into twelve divisions, based on their different flower forms.

Scilla campanulata, syn. Hyacinthoides hispanica

COMMON NAME: Spanish Bluebell
COLOR: Blue, pink, white
HEIGHT: 10 inches
FLOWERING SEASON: Late

This hardy bulb grows in shade and produces bell-shaped flowers. It is excellent for naturalizing.

Scilla siberica

COMMON NAME: Siberian Squill
COLOR: Blue
HEIGHT: 4–8 inches
FLOWERING SEASON: Early

This bulb grows well in full sun or partial shade and looks good with yellow daffodils.

Tulipa

CULTIVAR: 'Amethyst'
COMMON NAME: Tulip
COLOR: Purple
HEIGHT: 18 inches
FLOWERING SEASON: Late

This bulb produces rosy-lavender flowers with white accents (Parrot).

Tulipa

CULTIVAR: 'Angelique'
COMMON NAME: Tulip
COLOR: Light pink
HEIGHT: 20 inches
FLOWERING SEASON: Late

'Angelique' is of the most popular bulbs, producing fragrant double flowers (Double).

Tulipa

CULTIVAR: 'Apeldoorn'
COMMON NAME: Tulip
COLOR: Red
HEIGHT: 24 inches
FLOWERING SEASON: Mid-season

'Apeldoorn' is one of the best red tulips (Darwin).

Tulipa

CULTIVAR: 'Apricot Beauty'
COMMON NAME: Tulip
COLOR: Pale apricot
HEIGHT: 16 inches
FLOWERING SEASON: Mid-season

'Apricot Beauty' produces fragrant single flowers. It is good for forcing (Single).

Tulipa

CULTIVAR: 'Attila'
COMMON NAME: Tulip
COLOR: Purple
HEIGHT: 18 inches
FLOWERING SEASON: Mid-season

'Attila' produces egg-shaped blooms. It looks great with yellow or white narcissus and pansies (Triumph).

Tulipa

CULTIVAR: bakeri 'Lilac Wonder'
COMMON NAME: Tulip
COLOR: Lilac
HEIGHT: 6 inches
FLOWERING SEASON: Early

This tulip has a contrasting yellow base (Species).

Tulipa

CULTIVAR: batalinii 'Bright Gem'
COMMON NAME: Tulip
COLOR: Sulphur yellow
HEIGHT: 8 inches
FLOWERING SEASON: Mid-season

The color of this fragrant flower is affected by weather. In warm weather it looks bronze orange; in cooler weather it looks more yellowish (Species).

Tulipa

CULTIVAR: batalinii 'Red Gem'
COMMON NAME: Tulip
COLOR: Red
HEIGHT: 8 inches
FLOWERING SEASON: Mid-season

This bulb, known as red jewel, produces flowers with a pink glow (Species).

Tulipa

CULTIVAR: 'Bestseller'
COMMON NAME: Tulip
COLOR: Yellow orange
HEIGHT: 18 inches
FLOWERING SEASON: Early

'Bestseller' produces single flowers with a dusty rose accent (Single).

'Angelique' is one of the most popular tulips.

Tulipa

CULTIVAR: 'Black Diamond'
COMMON NAME: Tulip
COLOR: Light black
HEIGHT: 26 inches
FLOWERING SEASON: Late

The exterior of this tulip's blossom is dark reddish brown. At the edges, it is almost black (Darwin).

Tulipa

CULTIVAR: 'Blue Amiable'
COMMON NAME: Tulip
COLOR: Blue purple
HEIGHT: 24 inches
FLOWERING SEASON: Late

This tulip produces single flowers with exquisite shades of lilac.

Tulipa

CULTIVAR: 'Blue Bell'
COMMON NAME: Tulip
COLOR: Purple
HEIGHT: 20 inches
FLOWERING SEASON: Mid-season

This is a beautiful blue tulip (Lily cup).

'Blue Parrot' is sensitive to cold, wet weather.

Tulipa

CULTIVAR: 'Blue Parrot'
COMMON NAME: Tulip
COLOR: Blue purple
HEIGHT: 20 inches
FLOWERING SEASON: Late

Because this tulip is sensitive to cold, wet weather, plant in a protected spot (Parrot).

Tulipa

CULTIVAR: 'Blushing Lady'
COMMON NAME: Tulip
COLOR: White with pink edges
HEIGHT: 20 inches
FLOWERING SEASON: Late

'Blushing Lady' produces long-stemmed flowers. Plant it in mass (Lily).

Tulipa

CULTIVAR: 'Boccherini'
COMMON NAME: Tulip
COLOR: Blue purple
HEIGHT: 20 inches
FLOWERING SEASON: Mid-season

This tulip produces cup-shaped blooms (Triumph).

Tulipa

CULTIVAR: 'Burgundy Lace'
COMMON NAME: Tulip
COLOR: Burgundy
HEIGHT: 26 inches
FLOWERING SEASON: Late

This tulip produces long-lasting flowers (Fringed).

Tulipa

CULTIVAR: 'Carlton'
COMMON NAME: Tulip
COLOR: Red
HEIGHT: 24 inches
FLOWERING SEASON: Late

This bulb produces short sturdy stems (Double).

Tulipa

CULTIVAR: 'China Pink'
COMMON NAME: Tulip
COLOR: Pink
HEIGHT: 22 inches
FLOWERING SEASON: Mid-season

This tulip is an award winner (Lily).

Tulipa

CULTIVAR: 'Christmas Dream'
COMMON NAME: Tulip
COLOR: Light pink inside, fuchsia pink outside
HEIGHT: 12 inches
FLOWERING SEASON: Early

'Christmas Dream' is a strong, long-flowering bulb (Single).

Tulipa

CULTIVAR: 'Christmas Marvel'
COMMON NAME: Tulip
COLOR: Cherry pink
HEIGHT: 12 inches
FLOWERING SEASON: Early

This tulip produces fragrant flowers. It is good for forcing (Single).

Tulipa

CULTIVAR: 'Cistula'
COMMON NAME: Tulip
COLOR: Pale yellow
HEIGHT: 22 inches
FLOWERING SEASON: Mid-season

This tulip is quite elegant (Lily).

Tulipa

CULTIVAR: 'City of Vancouver'
COMMON NAME: Tulip
COLOR: Yellow, edged cream
HEIGHT: 28 inches
FLOWERING SEASON: Late

This tulip produces two-toned, oval-shaped flowers (Darwin).

Some of the different shapes of tulips

| Cup-shaped | Goblet-shaped | Fringed | Star-shaped |

Tulipa
CULTIVAR: 'Daydream'
COMMON NAME: Tulip
COLOR: Yellow changing to apricot
HEIGHT: 24 inches
FLOWERING SEASON: Mid-season

'Daydream' produces mildly fragrant flowers (Darwin).

Tulipa
CULTIVAR: 'Diana'
COMMON NAME: Tulip
COLOR: White
HEIGHT: 12 inches
FLOWERING SEASON: Mid-season

Some experts say this is the best white tulip (Single).

Tulipa
CULTIVAR: 'Douglas Baader'
COMMON NAME: Tulip
COLOR: Pale pink, apricot
HEIGHT: 14 inches
FLOWERING SEASON: Late

This flower has an ivory white base with exquisite rose-apricot pastel blooms (Single).

Tulipa
CULTIVAR: 'Dreaming Maid'
COMMON NAME: Tulip
COLOR: Lavender pink with white edge
HEIGHT: 16 inches
FLOWERING SEASON: Mid-season

'Dreaming Maid' flowers deepen in color as they mature (Triumph).

Tulipa
CULTIVAR: 'Elegant Lady'
COMMON NAME: Tulip
COLOR: Cream with pink
HEIGHT: 20 inches
FLOWERING SEASON: Mid-season

'Elegant Lady' produces a good cut flower. It is a favorite (Lily).

Tulipa
CULTIVAR: 'Elizabeth Arden'
COMMON NAME: Tulip
COLOR: Reddish orange with violet
HEIGHT: 24 inches
FLOWERING SEASON: Mid-season

This tulip is another favorite (Darwin).

Tulipa
CULTIVAR: 'Esther'
COMMON NAME: Tulip
COLOR: Glowing pink
HEIGHT: 22 inches
FLOWERING SEASON: Late

'Esther' is one of the best pink tulips. It is good for indoor forcing and is an Award of Merit winner (Single).

Tulipa
CULTIVAR: 'Fringed Elegance'
COMMON NAME: Tulip
COLOR: Pale yellow
HEIGHT: 28 inches
FLOWERING SEASON: Late

'Fringed Elegance' has fringed flowers with purple anthers (Fringed).

Tulipa
CULTIVAR: 'Ganders Rhapsody'
COMMON NAME: Tulip
COLOR: Light pink
HEIGHT: 28 inches
FLOWERING SEASON: Late

This tulip's unusual coloring changes with age (Triumph).

Tulipa
CULTIVAR: 'Georgette'
COMMON NAME: Tulip
COLOR: Yellow with red edge
HEIGHT: 24 inches
FLOWERING SEASON: Late

This tulip is multiflowered, producing at least four flowers per stem (Multiflowered).

Tulipa
CULTIVAR: 'Golden Apeldoorn'
COMMON NAME: Tulip
COLOR: Yellow gold
HEIGHT: 24 inches
FLOWERING SEASON: Mid-season

This tulip is good for mass plantings (Darwin).

Tulipa
CULTIVAR: 'Greenland'
COMMON NAME: Tulip
COLOR: Pink with green
HEIGHT: 16 inches
FLOWERING SEASON: Late

This tulip is also known as Groenland (Viridiflora).

Tulipa
CULTIVAR: 'Gudoshnik'
COMMON NAME: Tulip
COLOR: Yellow with orange
HEIGHT: 24 inches
FLOWERING SEASON: Mid-season

This tulip's colors range from red to yellow to rose (Darwin).

Tulipa
CULTIVAR: 'Happy Family'
COMMON NAME: Tulip
COLOR: Pink
HEIGHT: 18 inches
FLOWERING SEASON: Late

'Happy Family' is multiflowered and good for forcing (Multiflowered).

Tulipa
CULTIVAR: 'Hocus Pocus'
COMMON NAME: Tulip
COLOR: Yellow with red splash
HEIGHT: 24 inches
FLOWERING SEASON: Late

This tulip has some of the largest blossoms (Lily).

Tulipa
CULTIVAR: 'Jewel of Spring'
COMMON NAME: Tulip
FLOWERING SEASON: Mid-season
HEIGHT: 24 inches
COLOR: Pale yellow

This tulip is a five-time award winner (Darwin).

Tulipa
CULTIVAR: 'Kingsblood'
COMMON NAME: Tulip
FLOWERING SEASON: Late
HEIGHT: 25 inches
COLOR: Cherry red with scarlet margins

This tulip grows well and is one of the best reds (Single).

Tulipa
CULTIVAR: 'Lilac Perfection'
COMMON NAME: Tulip
FLOWERING SEASON: Late
HEIGHT: 20 inches
COLOR: Purple

'Lilac Perfection' produces large, double rose-like blooms (Double).

Pansies, narcissus, arabis, and tulips produce a lush bed of color and texture.

Tulipa
CULTIVAR: 'Mariette'
COMMON NAME: Tulip
FLOWERING SEASON: Late
HEIGHT: 22 inches
COLOR: Rose

'Mariette' is one of the most award-winning lily-flowering tulips (Lily).

Tulipa
CULTIVAR: 'Menton'
COMMON NAME: Tulip
FLOWERING SEASON: Late
HEIGHT: 28 inches
COLOR: Pink

'Menton' features varying shades of rose pink with muted apricot-pink edges (Single).

Tulipa
CULTIVAR: 'Modern Style'
COMMON NAME: Tulip
COLOR: White with purple
HEIGHT: 22 inches
FLOWERING SEASON: Mid-season

This tulip produces multiple flowers that can turn all purple (Multiflowered).

Tulipa
CULTIVAR: 'Mount Tacoma'
COMMON NAME: Tulip
COLOR: White
HEIGHT: 20 inches
FLOWERING SEASON: Late

This glistening white tulip is long lasting and fragrant (Double/Peony).

Tulipa
CULTIVAR: 'Mrs. J. T. Sheepers'
COMMON NAME: Tulip
COLOR: Yellow
HEIGHT: 24 inches
FLOWERING SEASON: Mid-season

This tulip is considered one of the most perfect (Single).

Tulipa
CULTIVAR: 'New Design'
COMMON NAME: Tulip
COLOR: Cream with pink
HEIGHT: 22 inches
FLOWERING SEASON: Mid-season

'New Design' features variegated foliage (Triumph).

Tulipa
CULTIVAR: 'Olympic Flame'
COMMON NAME: Tulip
COLOR: Red flame on yellow
HEIGHT: 24 inches
FLOWERING SEASON: Mid-season

'Olympic Flame' produces yellow flowers with red flames, reminiscent of the Olympic torch (Darwin).

Tulipa
CULTIVAR: 'Orange Bouquet'
COMMON NAME: Tulip
COLOR: Orange red
HEIGHT: 20 inches
FLOWERING SEASON: Mid-season

This tulip produces multiple flowers with a yellow base (Multiflowered).

Tulipa
CULTIVAR: 'Orange Favorite'
COMMON NAME: Tulip
COLOR: Orange
HEIGHT: 20 inches
FLOWERING SEASON: Late

This tulip is sweetly scented (Parrot).

Tulipa
CULTIVAR: 'Oxford'
COMMON NAME: Tulip
COLOR: Red with yellow base
HEIGHT: 24 inches
FLOWERING SEASON: Mid-season

'Oxford' has sturdy stems (Darwin).

'Olympic Flame' resembles the Olympic torch.

Tulipa
CULTIVAR: 'Peer Gynt'
COMMON NAME: Tulip
COLOR: Rose pink
HEIGHT: 18 inches
FLOWERING SEASON: Mid-season

This tulip produces immense blooms (Triumph).

Tulipa
CULTIVAR: 'Pink Emperor'
COMMON NAME: Tulip
COLOR: Pinkish red with yellow base
HEIGHT: 14 inches
FLOWERING SEASON: Early

'Pink Emporer' makes a magnificent cut flower (Fosteriana or Emperor).

Tulipa
CULTIVAR: 'Pink Impression'
COMMON NAME: Tulip
COLOR: Deep pink
HEIGHT: 22 inches
FLOWERING SEASON: Mid-season

'Pink Impression' produces large, long-lasting blooms (Darwin).

Tulipa
CULTIVAR: 'Polychroma,' 'Biflora'
COMMON NAME: Tulip
COLOR: White with violet and yellow
HEIGHT: 5 inches
FLOWERING SEASON: Early

This tulip produces fragrant star-shaped flowers (Species).

'Queen of Night' is considered the best of the "black tulips."

'Red Emperor' is a fiery-red early bloomer.

Tulipa
CULTIVAR: 'President Kennedy'
COMMON NAME: Tulip
COLOR: Yellow with orange
HEIGHT: 24 inches
FLOWERING SEASON: Mid-season

'President Kennedy' produces spectacular garden displays (Darwin).

Tulipa
CULTIVAR: 'Queen of Night'
COMMON NAME: Tulip
COLOR: Dark maroon, almost black
HEIGHT: 24 inches
FLOWERING SEASON: Late

This tulip was christened in 1944. It is considered the best of the "black" tulips. Its bloom looks velvety maroon (Single).

Tulipa
CULTIVAR: 'Red Emperor' ('Mme. Lefeber')
COMMON NAME: Tulip
COLOR: Fire red
HEIGHT: 14 inches
FLOWERING SEASON: Early

This fiery red tulip has won many awards (Fosteriana or Emperor).

Tulipa
CULTIVAR: 'Red Georgette'
COMMON NAME: Tulip
COLOR: Red
HEIGHT: 18 inches
FLOWERING SEASON: Late

'Red Georgette' produces multiple egg-shaped flowers (Multiflowering).

Tulipa
CULTIVAR: 'Red Riding Hood'
COMMON NAME: Tulip
COLOR: Carmine red
HEIGHT: 12 inches
FLOWERING SEASON: Early

'Red Riding Hood' is very popular (Greigii).

Tulipa
CULTIVAR: 'Red Shine'
COMMON NAME: Tulip
COLOR: Red with white base
HEIGHT: 22 inches
FLOWERING SEASON: Late

Plant 'Red Shine' with 'White Triumphator' (Lily).

Tulipa
CULTIVAR: 'Renown'
COMMON NAME: Tulip
COLOR: Rose
HEIGHT: 26 inches
FLOWERING SEASON: Late

This tulip is a great performer (Single).

Tulipa
CULTIVAR: 'Salmon Jewel'
COMMON NAME: Tulip
COLOR: Reddish orange with purple outside
HEIGHT: 24 inches
FLOWERING SEASON: Late

This stately tulip produces beautiful blooms (Triumph).

Tulipa
CULTIVAR: 'Shirley'
COMMON NAME: Tulip
COLOR: Purple with white edges
HEIGHT: 24 inches
FLOWERING SEASON: Late

'Shirley' makes an excellent cut flower. As its flowers age, the purple deepens (Triumph).

Tulipa
CULTIVAR: 'Sorbet'
COMMON NAME: Tulip
COLOR: White streaked with rose color
HEIGHT: 26 inches
FLOWERING SEASON: Mid-season

'Sorbet' is a beautiful five-time award winner (Single).

Tulipa
CULTIVAR: 'Spring Green'
COMMON NAME: Tulip
COLOR: White with green
HEIGHT: 16 inches
FLOWERING SEASON: Mid-season

This ivory white, long-lasting tulip has soft green featherings (Viridiflora).

Tulipa
CULTIVAR: 'Sweet Harmony'
COMMON NAME: Tulip
COLOR: Cream edge on yellow
HEIGHT: 26 inches
FLOWERING SEASON: Late

This tulip's long-lasting flowers have an unusual color (Darwin).

Tulipa
CULTIVAR: 'Sweet Lady'
COMMON NAME: Tulip
COLOR: Apricot pink
HEIGHT: 6 inches
FLOWERING SEASON: Early

'Sweet Lady' has striped leaves and long-lasting blooms (Greigii).

Tulipa
CULTIVAR: 'Sweetheart'
COMMON NAME: Tulip
COLOR: Ivory white with light yellow markings
HEIGHT: 20 inches
FLOWERING SEASON: Mid-season

'Sweetheart' is one of the most beautiful varieties (Fosteriana).

Tulipa
CULTIVAR: 'Temple of Beauty'
COMMON NAME: Tulip
COLOR: Salmon rose
HEIGHT: 28 inches
FLOWERING SEASON: Late

This tulip produces large blossoms (Lily).

Tulipa
CULTIVAR: 'Texas Flame'
COMMON NAME: Tulip
COLOR: Yellow with red
HEIGHT: 22 inches
FLOWERING SEASON: Late

This tulip can fall over but is a real eye-catcher (Parrot).

Tulipa
CULTIVAR: 'Toronto'
COMMON NAME: Tulip
COLOR: Reddish orange
HEIGHT: 12–14 inches
FLOWERING SEASON: Mid-season

'Toronto' tulips are multiflowering and feature marked and mottled foliage (Greigii).

Tulipa
CULTIVAR: 'White Triumphator'
COMMON NAME: Tulip
COLOR: White
HEIGHT: 22 inches
FLOWERING SEASON: Late

'White Triumphator' makes a great cut flower and is one of the best white tulips (Lily).

Tulipa
CULTIVAR: 'Yellow Present'
COMMON NAME: Tulip
COLOR: Pale yellow
HEIGHT: 14 inches
FLOWERING SEASON: Mid-season

This tulip is short but strong (Triumph).

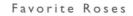

Favorite

Roses

Abraham Darby (R. 'Auscot')

TYPE: English Rose
COLOR: Pink, apricot

This David Austin Rose resists disease, blooms continually, and has a good fruity fragrance. It can grow up to ten feet as a climber or up to five feet as a bush.

Angel Face

TYPE: Floribunda
COLOR: Deep lavender

This continual bloomer has a strong heady fragrance. It grows two to three feet high.

Carefree Beauty (R. 'Audace')

TYPE: Landscape
COLOR: Rose pink

This repeat bloomer resists disease, grows up to six feet tall, and produces good rose hips in the fall.

Shrub roses, such as Joseph's Coat, *produce bounteous clusters of color.*

Different flower forms of roses

Flat

Cupped

Rounded

High-centered and urn-shaped

Rosette-shaped

Quartered rosette

Charlotte Armstrong

TYPE: Hybrid Tea

COLOR: Deep pink to light red

This repeat bloomer prefers the cool conditions of spring and fall, resists disease, and has a strong fragrance.

Cherish, syn. R. 'Jacsal'

TYPE: Floribunda

COLOR: Light pink

This continual bloomer resists disease and grows three to four feet high. Plant stays in tight compact form.

Eden

TYPE: Climber

COLOR: Blend of pink, cream, and yellow

This plant not only resists disease but also tolerates poor soil. It grows as high as eight feet, and continually produces fragrant blooms.

The Fairy

TYPE: Polyanthas

COLOR: Pink

This continual bloomer is a compact spreading plant that grows two to three feet high.

Great Century

TYPE: Hybrid Tea

COLOR: Salmon

Great Century has large blooms with a medium fragrance.

Green Ice

TYPE: Miniature Rose

COLOR: Soft green buds opening to white blossoms

This continual bloomer grows to a foot high, producing blooms with a unique color. It grows only in partial shade or morning sun.

Gruss an Aachen

TYPE: Floribunda
COLOR: Creamy white to pale pink

This rose, which grows to 2½ feet high and produces blooms with a light fragrance, can tolerate some shade.

Heritage

TYPE: English Rose
COLOR: Pink apricot

This David Austin Rose is a continual bloomer that grows four to five feet high and produces blooms with a lemon scent. It has few thorns and can be grown in partial shade.

Joseph's Coat

TYPE: Shrub
COLOR: Cherry red, blended with gold

This vigorous, moderately fragrant rose grows up to four feet high and three feet across.

Little Sizzler

TYPE: Miniature Rose
COLOR: Crimson

This miniature rose grows only to about eighteen inches high.

Nauvoo Rose

TYPE: Heritage Rose
COLOR: Red

This two-foot-high rose, according to history, is a transplant from Nauvoo, where it was introduced before 1847.

New Dawn

TYPE: Climber
COLOR: Silvery, pale pink

New Dawn blooms heavily in June with fragrant, intermittent blooms throughout the summer. It is one of the best climbers, reaching to twenty feet. It can tolerate a partially shaded site.

Sheer Bliss

TYPE: Hybrid Tea

COLOR: White with a hint of pale pink

Sheer Bliss is a repeat bloomer that produces good cut flowers with a strong fragrance. It resists disease and grows three to seven feet high.

Suzy Q

TYPE: Miniature Rose

COLOR: Pink

This miniature rose is a repeat bloomer. It is a good, compact plant for small gardens.

Sweet Juliet

TYPE: English Rose

COLOR: Apricot

This repeat bloomer grows from five inches to six feet high.

'The Fairy' yields continual blooms in front of the Lion House.

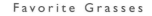

Favorite

Grasses

Briza media

COMMON NAME: Quaking Grass, Trembling Grass, Rattlesnake Grass
HEIGHT: 24–36 inches
WIDTH: 12 inches
LIGHT: Sun–partial shade
SOIL: Well-drained soil
FLOWERING SEASON: May–July

This perennial variety has flowers that appear in the shape of a rattle-snake's rattles. It tolerates hot weather but needs regular water.

Calamagrostis acutiflora

CULTIVAR: 'Karl Foerster'
COMMON NAME: Feather Reed Grass
HEIGHT: 5–6 feet
WIDTH: 2 feet
LIGHT: Partial shade–sun
SOIL: Moist, rich soil
FLOWERING SEASON: July–Sept.

This is a clump-forming grass with bronze flower plumes that turn to tan. In the early spring, cut all its foliage down. This grass has good winter interest.

Calamagrostis arundinacea

COMMON NAME: Korean Feather Reed Grass
HEIGHT: 3–4 feet
WIDTH: 18–24 inches
LIGHT: Sun–partial shade
SOIL: Moist soil
FLOWERING SEASON: Sept.

This clump-forming grass has glossy green leaves and feathery silver gray flowers, which last into the winter. Cut flowers are popular in fresh and dried arrangements.

Carex grayi

COMMON NAME: Gray's Sedge
HEIGHT: 2 feet
WIDTH: 2 feet
LIGHT: Partial shade–sun
SOIL: Well drained, moist soil
FLOWERING SEASON: June–Sept.

This perennial grass has green flowers that turn to star-shaped seed heads. It is good for flower arranging.

Cortaderia selloana

COMMON NAME: Pampas Grass
HEIGHT: 8–10 feet
WIDTH: 6 feet
LIGHT: Sun
SOIL: Well-drained, fertile soil
FLOWERING SEASON: Aug.–Sept.

This perennial grass has tall silvery flower plumes that provide winter interest. In the early spring, cut all foliage down.

Deschampsia caespitosa

CULTIVAR: 'Northern Lights'
COMMON NAME: Tufted Hair Grass
HEIGHT: 24 inches
WIDTH: 24 inches
LIGHT: Sun–partial shade
SOIL: Dry to slightly moist soil
FLOWERING SEASON: June–Sept.

This perennial grass has many delicate, airy flowers. Cut down foliage in the early spring.

Festuca glauca

COMMON NAME: Blue Fescue, Gray Fescue
HEIGHT: 12 inches
WIDTH: 10 inches
LIGHT: Sun
SOIL: Well-drained, dry, moderately fertile soil
FLOWERING SEASON: June–Aug.

This bluish perennial grass is good for edging. Divide it every three years to maintain vigor and color.

Melinis nerviglumis

COMMON NAME: Pink Crystals, Ruby Grass
HEIGHT: 2–3 feet
WIDTH: 2–3 feet
LIGHT: Sun–partial shade
SOIL: Well-drained, fertile soil
FLOWERING SEASON: Summer

This showy dwarf-flowering grass produces small clumps of bluish-green leaves adorned in the summer with iridescent pink flowers.

Miscanthus sinensis var. *purpurascens*

COMMON NAME: Autumn Red Fountain Grass
HEIGHT: 3–4 feet
WIDTH: 3–4 feet
LIGHT: Sun
SOIL: Well-drained, moist soil
FLOWERING SEASON: Sept.

Autumn red fountain grass has upright flower panicles and provides good winter interest. Cut the foliage down in early spring.

Panicum virgatum

CULTIVAR: 'Rehbraun'
COMMON NAME: Red Switch Grass
HEIGHT: 3–4 feet
WIDTH: 16 inches
LIGHT: Sun
SOIL: Well-drained soil
FLOWERING SEASON: Sept.

This perennial grass has tiny purple-green flowers and produces good winter interest. Cut the dried foliage in early spring.

Pennisetum setaceum

CULTIVAR: 'Atrosanguineum'
COMMON NAME: Fountain Grass
HEIGHT: 3½ feet
LIGHT: Sun
SOIL: Well-drained soil
FLOWERING SEASON: July–Sept.

This annual grass produces crimson-shaded flowers.

Feather reed and fountain grasses add interest to the plaza fountain area in both the summer and the winter.

Favorite

Trees and Shrubs

Berberis thunbergii

COMMON NAME: Japanese Barberry
VARIETY: 'Kobold,' 'Rosy gold'
LIGHT: Sun–partial shade
HEIGHT: 3 feet
WIDTH: 8 feet

This shrub is grown for the color of its variegated leaves, which turn from yellow to red in autumn. It flowers in the spring.

Buxus sempervirens

COMMON NAME: Boxwood
VARIETY: Many varieties
LIGHT: Sun–partial shade
HEIGHT: Dwarf to 15 feet
WIDTH: Varies as per variety

Boxwood, grown for its green foliage, does not tolerate wet conditions but is deer resistant.

Caragana aborescens

COMMON NAME: Siberian Pea Shrub
VARIETY: 'Pendula'
LIGHT: Full sun
HEIGHT: 5 feet
WIDTH: 4 feet

This shrub tolerates drought, salt, and wind. Its yellow flowers appear in the spring and early summer.

Caryopteris x clandonensis
VARIETY: 'Bluebeard'
LIGHT: Full sun–light shade
HEIGHT: 3 feet
WIDTH: 5 feet

This shrub produces blue flowers from late summer to early autumn. It does not like wet conditions, tolerates some drought, and prefers fertile soil.

Cornus sericea (stolonifera)
COMMON NAME: Red Twig Dogwood
LIGHT: Sun–partial shade
HEIGHT: 6 inches
WIDTH: 12 inches

This shrub produces white flowers in late spring and early summer and green leaves that turn reddish orange in autumn. It tolerates drought, moisture, air pollution, and some soil compaction.

Cotoneaster apiculatus
COMMON NAME: Cranberry Cotoneaster
LIGHT: Sun
HEIGHT: 3 feet
WIDTH: 8 feet

Cranberry cotoneaster produces red-tinged white flowers in the summer and leaves that turn red in autumn. It thrives in dry, sandy soil and does not tolerate permanently wet soils.

Daphne x burkwoodii
VARIETY: 'Carol Mackie'
LIGHT: Sun–partial shade
HEIGHT: 3 feet
WIDTH: 3 feet

This shrub produces leaves with white edges and, in late spring, fragrant flowers. It likes well-drained, fertile, moist soil.

Euonymus alatus
COMMON NAME: Burning Bush
VARIETY: Many varieties
LIGHT: Sun–light shade
HEIGHT: Up to 15 feet
WIDTH: 10 feet

Burning bush has green leaves that turn red in autumn. It's known for its fall color, comes in dwarf form, and likes well-drained soil.

Forsythia x intermedia
COMMON NAME: Forsythia
VARIETY: 'Northern Sun'
LIGHT: Sun–light shade
HEIGHT: 8 feet
WIDTH: 7–9 feet

Forsythia has green leaves and, in the early spring, yellow flowers. It can force stems indoors.

Hydrangea arborescens

COMMON NAME: Hills of Snow
VARIETY: 'Annabelle'
LIGHT: Full sun–partial shade
HEIGHT: 3 feet
WIDTH: 5 feet

This shrub produces white flowers and grows in moist, well-drained soil. Its flowers dry well for use in arrangements.

Ilex (serrata x verticillata)

COMMON NAME: Winterberry, Holly
VARIETY: 'Sparkleberry'
LIGHT: Sun–partial shade
HEIGHT: 15 feet
WIDTH: 12 feet

This female variety needs I. *Apollo* for pollination. It has dark green leaves and produces wonderful red berries in winter.

Mahonia aquifolium

COMMON NAME: Oregon Grapeholly
VARIETY: Many varieties
LIGHT: Full–partial shade
HEIGHT: 3 feet
WIDTH: 5 feet

Oregon grapeholly has green leaves that turn reddish purple in the late fall. It has yellow flowers in the spring and produces bluish black berries. It likes fertile, moist, well-drained soil.

Picea abies

COMMON NAME: Dwarf Norway
  Spruce
VARIETY: 'Little Gem'
LIGHT: Full sun–light shade
HEIGHT: 12 inches
WIDTH: 12 inches

This green, slow-growing, dwarf shrub has short needles and a flat top.

Picea omorika

COMMON NAME: Dwarf Serbian
  Spruce
VARIETY: 'Nana'
LIGHT: Sun
HEIGHT: 3 feet
WIDTH: 3 feet

'Nana' is the slow-growing dwarf form of this green shrub, which likes moist, well-drained, slightly acidic to neutral soil.

Picea pungens

COMMON NAME: Dwarf Colorado
  Spruce
VARIETY: 'Montgomery'
LIGHT: Full sun
HEIGHT: 5 feet
WIDTH: 3 feet

Dwarf Colorado spruce is the slow-growing form of this shrub, which has a conical shape and silvery gray-blue leaves. It likes deep, moist, slightly acidic, well-drained soil.

Pinus mugo

COMMON NAME: Dwarf Mountain
　　Pine
LIGHT: Full sun
HEIGHT: 8 feet
WIDTH: 15 feet

This spherically shaped green shrub grows only about 2½ inches per year. It likes well-drained soil.

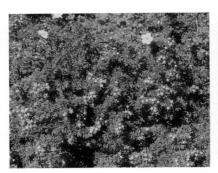

Potentilla fruticosa

COMMON NAME: Shrubby Cinquefoil
VARIETY: Many varieties
LIGHT: Full sun
HEIGHT: Varies
WIDTH: 5 feet

Yellow flowers usually appear on this shrub from spring to fall. It likes poor to moderately fertile, well-drained soil.

Spiraea x bumalda (japonica)

COMMON NAME: Gold Flame Spiraea
VARIETY: 'Goldflame' variety albiflora
LIGHT: Full sun
HEIGHT: 36 inches
WIDTH: 30 inches

This shrub's young bronze-red leaves turn bright yellow and then green. In the autumn, when it produces dark pink flowers, its leaves turn orange, red, and yellow. It likes fertile, well-drained soil.

Taxus

COMMON NAME: Yew
VARIETY: Many varieties
LIGHT: Sun–deep shade
HEIGHT: Up to 20 feet
WIDTH: Up to 20 feet

This shrub has dark-green needles. Plant it in well-drained, fertile soil, and prune it (not hard) in the summer and early autumn.

Viburnum carlesii

COMMON NAME: Koreanspice
　　Viburnium
LIGHT: Full sun–partial shade
HEIGHT: 6 feet
WIDTH: 6 feet

This shrub has green leaves that turn red in autumn. It produces fragrant pink and white flowers, and it likes well-drained, moist soil.

Viburnum plicatum f. tomentosum

COMMON NAME: Summer Snowflake
LIGHT: Full sun–partial shade
HEIGHT: 6 feet
WIDTH: 10 feet

This shrub produces white flowers in the late spring and early summer. It likes well-drained, moist soil.

Trees offer a complementary subtlety to many of the gardens on Temple Square.

More

Favorites

EASY-CARE PERENNIALS

The following flowers are generally considered to be low-maintenance plants—but only after becoming established in the garden. This is not an exhaustive list, but it represents some of the plants that have required relatively little maintenance on Temple Square. Some of these plants may need deadheading during their bloom time, and you may have to watch for slugs and snails. See the listing of perennials on pages 95–117 for more information about each plant.

Achillea tomentosa
Woolly Yarrow

Aconitum napellus
Monkshood

Ajuga
Bugleweed

Anemone x hybrida
Japanese Anemone

Aquilegia
Columbine

Arabis caucasica
Rock Cress

Armeria maritima
Sea Thrift

Aster frikartii
Aster

Aubrieta
False Rock Cress

Bergenia cordifolia
Elephant's Ears

Boltonia asteroides
Snowbank Boltonia

Brunnera macrophylla
Siberian Bugloss

Campanula
(all species) Bellflower

Centranthus ruber
Jupiter's Beard, Red Valerian, Keys of Heaven

Cimicifuga racemosa
Black Snakeroot, Black Cohosh

Cimicifuga simplex
Autumn Snakeroot

Coreopsis grandiflora
Tickseed

Corydalis lutea
Corydalis

Crocosmia
Montbretia

Digitalis purpurea
Common Foxglove

Doronicum cordatum
Leopard's Bane

Echinacea purpurea
Coneflower

Gaillardia x grandiflora
Blanket Flower

Galium odoratum
Sweet Woodruff

Gaura lindheimeri
Apple Blossom Grass

Geranium
'Johnson's Blue'
Cranesbill

Geranium sanguineum
Bloody Cranesbill

Helleborus orientalis
Lenten Rose

Hemerocallis
Daylily

Hesperis matronalis
Dame's Rocket

Hosta
Plantain Lily

Iberis sempervirens
Candytuft

Iris sibirica
Siberian Iris

Lamium maculatum
Spotted Deadnettle

Lavandula angustifolia
Lavender

Liatris
Gayfeather, Blazing Star

Lilium
Lily

Papaver orientale
Oriental Poppy

Penstemon barbatus
Beardlip Penstemon

Perovskia atriplicifolia
Russian Sage

Phlox paniculata
Garden Phlox

Platycodon grandiflorus
Balloon Flower

Primula auricula
Primrose

Pulmonaria officinalis
Lungwort

Rudbeckia fulgida
Black-eyed Susan

Rudbeckia hirta
Black-eyed Susan

Fountain grass adds elegance to a bed of geraniums and petunias.

Salvia nemorosa
Perennial Salvia

Saponaria ocymoides
Rock Soapwort

Scabiosa columbaria
Pincushion Flower

Sedum 'Herbstfreude'
Sedum

Solidago hybrids
Goldenrod

Trollius europaeus
Globeflower

Verbascum
Mullein

LONG-BLOOMING PERENNIALS

These plants bloom most of the season, especially when they are deadheaded.

Achillea
Yarrow

Aster frikartii
'Mönch'
Aster

Campanula persicifolia
Peach-leaved Bellflower

Coreopsis verticillata
'Moonbeam'
Thread-leaved Tickseed

Dianthus barbatus
Sweet William

Echinacea purpurea
Coneflower

Leucanthemum x superbum
'Snowcap'
Shasta Daisy

Monarda didyma
Bee Balm

Nepeta x faassenii
Cat Mint

Phlox paniculata
Garden Phlox

Rudbeckia fulgida
Black-eyed Susan

Salvia nemorosa
Perennial Salvia

Scabiosa columbaria
'Pink Mist'
Pincushion Flower

The Salt Lake Temple appears to be nestled among beds of coleus, geraniums, verbena, and scaevola.

PERENNIALS THAT DO NOT REQUIRE DEADHEADING

Astilbe x arendsii
Astilbe

Baptisia australis
False Indigo, Wild Blue Indigo

Boltonia asteroides
'Snowbank'
Snowbank Boltonia

Cimicifuga racemosa
Black Snakeroot, Black Cohosh

Clematis jackmanii
Clematis

Clematis montana
'Alba'
Clematis

Crocosmia
'Lucifer'
Montbretia

Filipendula rubra
Queen-of-the-prairie

Helianthus annuus
Sunflower

Hypericum calycinum
Aaron's Beard, Rose of Sharon

Papaver orientale
Oriental Poppy

Perovskia atriplicifolia
Russian Sage

Sedum 'Herbstfreude'
'Autumn Joy'
Sedum

Thermopsis caroliniana (I. villosa)
Carolina Lupine

PERENNIALS TO CUT BACK

The following perennials should be cut back before they bloom. Cutting back produces shorter, more compact plants, and can delay blooms.

Achillea millefolium
Yarrow
Cut back by one-half to two-thirds in early May.

Aconitum napellus
Monkshood
Cut back by one-half when this plant is about 18 inches tall.

Alcea (Althaea) rosea
Hollyhock
Cut back by one-half to three-quarters once or twice in the early spring before it begins flowering.

Artemisia schmidtiana
Wormwood
Cut back by one-half in June to produce a more compact plant.

Aster frikartii
Aster
Cut back by one-half in May to prevent lanky stems.

Aster novi-belgii
Michaelmas Daisy
Cut back by one-half in mid-June and again in late July. Blooms will come on later, but the plant will have a nice rounded shape and won't need to be staked.

Boltonia asteroids
Snowbank Boltonia
Cut back by one-half during the first two weeks of June and again in July. This will result in a later bloom time.

Echinacea purpurea
Coneflower
Cut back by one-half in the first two weeks of June.

Gaura lindheimeri
Apple Blossom Grass
Cut back by one-half in the first two weeks of June, when the plant is about fifteen inches tall. Cut back again by one-quarter in July.

Helianthemum
Sun Rose
Cut back one-quarter in April or May to create denser growth and reduce height.

Hypericum calycinum
Aaron's Beard, Rose of Sharon
Cut to about six inches in the early spring every other year to increase density and maintain vigor.

Black-eyed Susan gives a yellow vibrancy to this Temple Square garden.

Lavandula angustifolia
Lavender
Cut back to six inches every few years in early June. Shape the plant into a mound.

Linum perenne
Perennial Flax
Cut plant back by one-half in early May to increase fullness.

Lobelia cardinalis
Cardinal Flower
Cut back in June before blooms appear to produce a more compact plant.

Monarda didyma
Bee Balm
Cut back in May when the plant is about a foot tall.

Cutting back again in early June will delay flowering but prolong bloom time into August.

Perovskia atriplicifolia
Russian Sage
Cut back to about six inches from the ground in early spring. Cut back again by one-half when the plant is about a foot tall.

Phlox paniculata
Garden Phlox
Cut back by one-half in early June to delay flowering and produce a shorter, more compact plant.

Physostegia virginiana
Obedient Plant
Cut back by one-half in May to produce a more compact plant. Cutting back will prevent floppy stems, especially in shadier areas.

Platycodon grandiflorus
Balloon Flower
Cut back by one-half in late May or early June to produce a more compact plant.

Rudbeckia hirta
Black-eyed Susan
Cut back by one-half in late May to produce a more compact plant.

Sedum 'Herbstfreude'
Sedum
Pinch back to about four inches when the plant is about eight inches tall—usually in June. Pinching is preferred over cutting so that stems are stronger during winter months.

Solidago hybrids
Goldenrod
Cut back by one-half in early June to produce more compact growth. Cutting back will delay flowering by a month.

Veronica spicata
Spike Speedwell
Cut back by about six inches in early June to produce a more compact plant. Flowering will be delayed a few weeks.

SHADE-LOVING PLANTS

Annuals

Begonia semperflorens
Fibrous Begonia

Brachyscome iberidifolia
Swan River Daisy

Browallia speciosa
Bush Violet

Coleus (Solenostemon)
'Wizard Series'
Coleus, Painted Nettle

Hypoestes phyllostachya
Polka-dot Plant

Impatiens
Impatiens

Lobelia erinus
Lobelia

Nephrolepis exaltata
Boston Fern

Nicotiana alata
Flowering Tobacco

Torenia fournieri
'Clown Series,' 'Summer Wave Series'
Wishbone Flower

Perennials

Aconitum napellus
Monkshood

Ajuga
Bugleweed

Alchemilla mollis
Lady's Mantle

Anemone x hybrida
Japanese Anemone

Aquilegia
'McKana Hybrids'
Columbine

Aruncus dioicus
Goatsbeard

Asarum europaeum
Wild Ginger

Astilbe x arendsii
Astilbe

Bergenia cordifolia
Elephant's Ears

Brunnera macrophylla
Siberian Bugloss

Campanula persicifolia
Peach-leaved Bellflower

Campanula portenschlagiana
Dalmatian Bellflower

Campanula poscharskyana
Serbian Bellflower

Campanula pyramidalis
Chimney Bellflower

Cimicifuga racemosa
Black Snakeroot, Black Cohosh

Cimicifuga simplex
Autumn Snakeroot

Clematis jackmanii
Clematis

Clematis montana
Clematis

Convallaria majalis
Lily-of-the-valley

Corydalis lutea
Corydalis

Dicentra spectabilis
Bleeding Heart

Digitalis purpurea
Common Foxglove

Doronicum cordatum
Leopard's Bane

Epimedium alpinum
Barrenwort

Galium odoratum
Sweet Woodruff

Helleborus orientalis
Lenten Rose

Heuchera micrantha
'Bressingham Hybrids'
Coral Bells

Heuchera sanguinea
'Splendens'
Coral Bells

Hosta
Plantain Lily

Lamium maculatum
Spotted Deadnettle

Ligularia dentata
Golden Groundsel

Lobelia cardinalis
Cardinal Flower

Lysimachia clethroides
Gooseneck Loosestrife

Meconopsis cambrica
Welsh Poppy

Mertensia pulmonarioides
Virginia Bluebells

Monarda didyma
Bee Balm

Myosotis sylvatica
Forget-me-not

Pachysandra terminalis
'Silver Edge,' 'Green Sheen'
Japanese Spurge

Polemonium caeruleum
Jacob's Ladder

Polygonatum biflorum
Solomon's Seal

An array of summer annuals complements the sculptural grouping Joyful Moment.

Primula auricula
Primrose

Pulmonaria officinalis
'Sissinghurst White'
Lungwort

Sanguinaria canadensis
Bloodroot

Thalictrum aquilegiifolium
Meadow Rue

Thalictrum rochebruneanum
'Lavender Mist'
Meadow Rue

Tiarella wherryi
Foam Flower

Vinca minor
Creeping Myrtle, Dwarf Periwinkle

PLANTS FOR DRY, HOT GARDENS

Annuals

Agapanthus
Lily-of-the-Nile

Calendula officinalis
Pot Marigold, English Marigold

Catharanthus roseus
Vinca

Dyssodia tenuiloba (Thymophylla tenuiloba)
Dahlberg Daisy, Golden Fleece

Eustoma grandiflorum
'Mermaid,' 'Heidi,' 'Lisa'
Texas Bluebell

Gazania rigens
Treasure Flower

Helianthus annuus
Sunflower

Lantana camara
Lantana, Shrub Verbena

Portulaca grandiflora
Moss Rose

Sanvitalia procumbens
Creeping Zinnia

Verbena canadensis
'Homestead Purple'
Rose Vervain

Zinnia haageana
'Pinwheel series'
Zinnia

Perennials

Achillea
'Moonshine'
Yarrow

Arabis caucasica
Rock Cress

Artemisia schmidtiana
'Silver Mound'
Wormwood

Asclepias tuberosa
Butterfly Weed

Boltonia asteroides
'Snowbank'
Snowbank Boltonia

Centranthus ruber
Jupiter's Beard, Red Valerian, Keys of Heaven

Coreopsis rosea
Tickseed

Coreopsis verticillata
'Moonbeam,' 'Zagreb'
Thread-leaved Tickseed

Dianthus barbatus
Sweet William

Dianthus deltoides
Maiden Pinks

Echinacea purpurea
Coneflower

Gaillardia x grandiflora
Blanket Flower

Gaura lindheimeri
'Whirling Butterflies,' 'Siskiyou pink'
Apple Blossom Grass

Helianthemum
Sun Rose

Hemerocallis
Daylily

Lavandula angustifolia
Lavender

Liatris
Gayfeather, Blazing Star

Linum perenne
Perennial Flax

Oenothera missouriensis
Missouri Evening Primrose

Oenothera speciosa
Pink Evening Primose

Penstemon barbatus
'Elfin Pink'
Beardlip Penstemon

Perovskia atriplicifolia
Russian Sage

Rudbeckia fulgida
Black-eyed Susan

Salvia nemorosa
Perennial Salvia

Sedum 'Herbstfreude'
'Autumn Joy'
Sedum

Sedum kamtschaticum
Stonecrop

Sidalcea malviflora

Stately statues of Joseph Smith and Hyrum Smith stand between gardens of pansies and tulips.

'Loveliness'
Checkerbloom, Mallow

Solidago hybrids
Goldenrod

Stachys byzantina
Lambs' Ears

Thymus
Thyme

Chapter 10

Gardening Resources

INTERNET

Y ou can find an explosion of gardening resources on the internet. If you do not have computer internet access at home, chances are your public library does. The internet is filled with resources to help you purchase gardening tools, locate hard-to-find plants, find articles on almost every gardening subject imaginable, and get information on clubs organized on specific classifications of plants (The Hosta Society, for example). Here are a few websites to get you started:

- www.GardenNet.com (features several links to other gardening sites)
- www.bulb.com
- www.garden.com
- www.webbound.com (see the links under Gardens)
- www.almanac.com

If you are searching for a particular plant, you can also go to a search engine, such as Google (www.google.com), and type in the name of the plant. Remember that web addresses can change, and be sure your computer is set up with an antivirus program.

BOOKS, MAGAZINES, AND CATALOGS

Many books, magazines, and catalogs deal with gardening. The ones listed below are some of our favorites.

Books

The American Horticultural Society Flower Finder, by Jacqueline Heriteau and Andre Viette

The American Horticultural Society A-Z Encyclopedia of Garden Plants, edited by Christopher Brickell and Judith D. Zuk

Carrots Love Tomatoes and Roses Love Garlic, by Louise Riotte

100 English Roses for the American Garden, by Clair G. Martin

The Essential Gardener, by Derek Fell

Shocking Beauty, by Thomas Hobbs

Sunset Western Garden Book, edited by Kathleen N. Brenzel

The Undaunted Garden, by Lauren Springer

Colorful tulips surrounding the plaza fountain south of the Church Office Building welcome the spring.

The Well-Tended Perennial Garden, by Tracy
   DiSabato-Aust

Magazines

Country Gardens, 1716 Locust Street., Des Moines,
   IA, 50309-3023, (800) 677-0484, www.coun-
   tryhome.com

Country Living Gardens, P.O. Box 7335, Red Oak,
   IA, 51591, cgncustserv@hearstsc.com

Fine Gardening, 63 S. Main Street, Newton, CT,
   06470

Garden Gate, P.O. Box 37114, Boone, IA,
   50037–2114, www.gardengatemagazine.com

Gardens Illustrated, 3330 Pacific Avenue, Suite
   404, Virginia Beach, VA, 23451–2983, (888)
   410–9858, www.gardensillustrated.com

Horticulture, P.O. Box 5429, Boulder, CO,
   80323–1455

Catalogs

Andre Viette Farm and Nursery, P.O. Box 1109,
   Fisherville, VA, 22939, (540) 943–2315,
   www.viette.com

Brent & Becky's Bulbs, 7463 Heath Trail,
   Gloucester, VA, 23061, (804) 693–3966,
   www.brentandbeckysbulbs.com

Collector's Nursery, 16804 NE 102ⁿᵈ Avenue,
   Battleground, WA, 98604, (360) 574–3832

Dutch Gardens, U.S. Reservation Center, 144
   Intervale Road, Burlington, VT, 06401, (800)
   944–2250, www.dutchgardens.com

Forestfarm, 990 Tetherow Road, Williams, OR,
   97544–9599, www.forestfarm.com

Hardy Perennials, Russell Graham Purveyor of
   Plants, 4030 Eagle Crest Road, N.W., Salem,
   OR, 97304, (503) 362–1135

Heirloom Old Garden Roses, 24062 NE Riverside

Drive, St. Paul, OR, 97137, (503) 538–1576,
   www.heirloomroses.com

Heronswood Nursery, 7530 NE 288ᵗʰ Street,
   Kingston, WA, 98346–9502, (360) 297–4172

High Country Gardens, 2902 Rufina Street, Santa
   Fe, NM, 87505–2929, (800) 492–7885,
   www.highcountrygardens.com

High Country Roses, P.O. Box 148, 9122 E.
   Highway 40, Jensen, UT, 84035, (800) 552-
   2082, roses@easilink.com, www.highcountry-
   roses.com

John Scheepers, Inc., 23 Tulip Drive, P.O. Box 638,
   Bantam, CT, 06750–0638, (860) 567–0838,
   www.johnscheepers.com

McClure & Zimmerman, P.O. Box 368, Friesland,
   WI, 53935–0368. (800) 883–6998,
   www.mzbulb.com

Van Bourgondien, 245 Farmingdale Road, P.O. Box
   1000, Babylon, NY, 11702–9004, (800)
   622–9997, www.dutchbulbs.com

Van Dyck's, U.S. Reservation Center, P.O. Box 430,
   Brightwaters, NY, 11718–0430, (800)
   639–2452, www.vandycks.com

White Flower Farm, P.O. Box 50, Litchfield, CT,
   06759–0050, (800) 503–9624, www.white-
   flowerfarm.com

COUNTY EXTENSION AGENTS

Every state has an extension service that is
usually set up by counties. Each agency is the
educational arm of the U.S. Department of
Agriculture. The extension agency provides information on agriculture production, plants common
to the area, water conservation, soil testing, and
many other subjects. To find the extension agency
in your area, look in the local phone directory
under government listings by county. You will find
it listed under "County Extension Agency." To find

your local agency on the internet, go to
http://plantfacts.ohio-state.edu/

SOIL TESTING

We test the soil in the Temple Square gardens about every five years. You should also have your garden soil checked frequently. Your local county extension office has soil sample bags you can use to have your soil tested.

MASTER GARDENERS

The Master Gardener program began in Seattle in 1973. Its purpose is to train gardeners through forty hours of classroom training, courses, and hands-on experience, and another forty hours of service. The service portion of the requirement allows gardeners to help their local extension office answer questions, give lectures in the community, supervise information booths at fairs and home and garden shows, help maintain demonstration gardens, and assist at plant diagnostic clinics.

There are Master Gardener programs in more than forty states. In Utah, programs are offered in six counties. Check with your local extension agency for a listing of lectures and classes.

GARDEN GUIDES AT TEMPLE SQUARE

The garden guides at Temple Square give tours of the beautiful gardens on the Church Office Building block as well as on the roof of the Conference Center. They also go into the community, from Provo to Ogden, and give presentations on gardening. Subjects covered can range from a history of gardening in the Salt Lake Valley to garden design and maintenance, fertilizers, and soils. All presentations are free. Call (801) 240-5916

GARDEN TALKS IN THE PARK

Under the direction of the Temple Square Garden Guide office, a series of lectures on gardening are given in the Brigham Young Historic Park each Wednesday evening from June through August. Professionals, Master Gardeners, and those educated in various topics give hour-long lectures, which are free to the public. Call (801) 240-5916

UTELITE

Utelite is referred to in several chapters throughout the book. Labeled as Utelite Soil Conditioner, it is available at many Utah nurseries in bags or in bulk. For more information, call the Utelite Corporation in the Salt Lake area at (801) 467–2800, or visit www.utelite.com. Utelite Corporation is part of the Expanded Shale, Clay, and Slate Institute.

Index

Other photographs in the Favorite lists by the National Garden Bureau: Lobelia, 'Aqua Lavender,' Penstamen, 'Cambridge Mix,' Cathranthus, Hypoestes, 'Confetti Mix,' 'Ocimum Basil,' 'Purple Ruffles'; Perennial Plant Association: Perovskia, Russian Sage; All-America Selections: Cosmos, 'Sunny Red,' Sunflower, 'Soraya,' Calendula, 'Fiesta Gitana Superior Mix,' Nierembergia, Torenia, Marigold, Tagates, 'Honey Sophia'; Netherlands Flower Bulb Information Center: Red Pompom Dahlia 'Nescio,' 'Queen of the Night,' 'Fragrant Narcissis N. Cragford,' Tulip 'Angelique,' Tulip 'Black Parrot'; All American Rose Selections: Sheer Bliss, 'Hybrid Tea'; Diane Sagers: all other rose pictures; Jerry Goodspeed: Polemonium, Jacob's ladder; Brent Gledhill: Berberis Thunbergii, 'Kobold.' Also, Debbie Amundson, the Utah Botanical Center and Mary Garr.